FIELD PROJECTS IN ANTHROPOLOGY

• A STUDENT HANDBOOK

D1500542

Anthropologists John and Beatrice Whiting, who are directing a long-term study of childhood in Kenya. Photograph by Robert E. Daniels.

FIELD PROJECTS IN
ANTHROPOLOGY

- A Student Handbook

JULIA G. CRANE
University of North Carolina, Chapel Hill

MICHAEL V. ANGROSINO
University of South Florida, Tampa

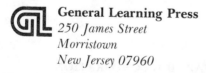

General Learning Press
250 James Street
Morristown
New Jersey 07960

Manufactured in the United States of America.

Published simultaneously in Canada.

Library of Congress Catalog Card Number 74-78017

ISBN 0-382-18033-X

PREFACE

Recently some of our undergraduate students have begun to ask, "How can I know whether or not I really want to be an anthropologist if I can't practice being one?" How indeed? Practicing anthropology may include many experiences, but fieldwork, in particular, is often considered a sort of "rite of passage," a necessary prerequisite for one to be considered a bona fide anthropologist. We feel it can also be important for anyone who wants to understand basic concepts and get a feeling for the anthropological perspective.

Throughout a long period in the development of anthropology, students who were almost ready to go into the field for their first large-scale research learned from their major professors some of the ideas and techniques that had proved useful to them and others with whom they had worked. On at least some campuses, an aura of mystery seems to have surrounded this process of learning that would only take place at the feet of a guru. Even when some courses on field methods were finally created, most were tailored for advanced graduate students.

During this period only a handful of books gave any useful insights. Fortunately, anthropologists are now beginning to write insightfully and candidly about their fieldwork experiences in many ethnographies. It is this spate of new information that has been invaluable in the writing of this book.

Field Projects in Anthropology is primarily for undergraduates and for beginning graduate students. It is not intended as a complete manual of field techniques. Because anthropologists work in many kinds of situations, in societies that differ greatly from one another, they must be flexible, often learning in their own particular field situations a great deal about what avenues of approach to follow, what questions to ask, what projective tests to use, what kinds of photographs to take, what conversations to record—and also what areas to carefully avoid or delay in exploring. It would, therefore, be impossible to find agreement among anthropologists that *any* particular collection of projects, however chosen, satisfactorily represented the most basic and essential aspects of field research. Complete coverage is not our real aim. Rather, our aim is to present a series of projects that represent some of the most commonly used data-collection techniques. In carrying out the projects, each student will learn something about how and when to apply such techniques, or variants of them, in the field situation.

Students using the projects in this book under the supervision of their instructors will not merely pick up a few suggestions and specific facts about fieldwork techniques, but they will experience the special sense of excitement and personal satisfaction that comes from having established significant human relationships with others whose lifeways are different from their own, as well as having perceptively and carefully gleaned insights into their cultural perspectives.

The following fourteen projects represent areas of inquiry that have been traditional foci of anthropological research. For each topic we suggest a "method" or "data-collecting tool" by which the topic may profitably be investigated. This is to imply neither that the topic cannot be investigated by other means nor that the method cannot be used to investigate other topics. Moreover, it is obvious that no one research tool is self-sufficient. A good ethnography makes use of as many such tools as possible to gather a more nearly complete set of data about the culture being studied.

We believe that in the descriptions of the methods and in the selected bibliographies for each chapter we have left sufficient leeway for the student, working under the knowledgeable guidance of his or her instructor, to experiment, modify, or amplify the method to suit his or her own research needs. The selected bibliographies are composed of items that we have found useful in describing the topic area and in planning the project, but they are not in any way exhaustive compilations of all extant literature in any of the selected areas of study. The entries are mainly to be used as initial points of reference, and they are, for the most part, those works that are most readily available and most directly relevant to the suggested projects. The student, on his or her own initiative or under the direction of the instructor, is encouraged to go beyond these basic references insofar as time, energy, and research potential permit.

Although we present the projects in what seems to us to be a logical progression, we realize that the individual instructor must adapt the format of the book to his own particular course outline. In general, though, the following comments may be of use in planning course work.

The first four projects are designed so that even a beginning student in anthropology could reasonably carry them out. Each of them represents a basic area of field research and would be useful also as an early project in a more advanced field methods course. The beginning student can also get a feel for the "how-to" aspects of anthropology by trying his or her hand at these basic tasks.

Projects 5 through 9 are somewhat more complex in nature. They require periodic observations or other data-gathering sessions on the part of the student. Ideally, they should be started fairly early in the semester to give the student sufficient time to do full justice to the research.

Projects 10 through 14 can be made as complex or as basic as the instructor feels appropriate. Each can constitute a short-term effort, although more advanced students can make them the bases of more detailed, time-consuming studies. Project 14, in particular, may be used as a general summation of many methods and concepts in anthropology in the field.

It should be noted that some of the projects may profitably be done in tandem; for example, combining the photographic series (Project 13) with the observation of ritual (Project 5). We suggest that the instructor and student look over the project descriptions at the beginning of the course in order to be sure of ways in which efforts may be combined.

Although anthropology is a serious scholarly discipline, we feel that it is also highly enjoyable. We hope that this book will help the student channel his or her natural curiosity about the customs and lifestyle of other peoples into anthropology's scientific framework.

ACKNOWLEDGMENTS

Throughout the course of our writing, we have constantly solicited the comments and criticisms of our undergraduate and graduate students, and of our colleagues. We acknowledge their help with deep appreciation, while claiming as our own the responsibility for any shortcomings in the book. Our research assistants — who sometimes also served as our severest critics — were Barbara Downey Brick, Beverley Hurlbert, Linda Oldham Lester, and Isabel Terry Rutter.

We are deeply indebted to those upon whose work we have drawn, some of whom not only gave permission for us to use their ideas but assisted us in doing so. They include Professors Donald L. Brockington and Dorothea C. Leighton of the University of North Carolina at Chapel Hill and David and Gloria Johnson of North Carolina Agricultural and Technical University.

We have been fortunate indeed in having the help of Charles Mohler, William Sommerfield, Susan Horowitz and Bonnie Monfort Bopp of General Learning Press, whose expertise and sensitivity in the realm of books were of great assistance, and whose warmth and human understanding have been supportive in periods of personal crisis, as well as over the long haul of preparing, writing, and revising the book.

CONTENTS

CONTENTS

INTRODUCTION

Within cultural anthropology there are three subfields: archaeology, linguistics, and ethnology. Ethnology, the subfield with
which we are most concerned in this book, is the "science of
peoples, their cultures, and life histories as groups" [Kroeber
1948, p. 5]. Like anthropology in general, ethnology is comparative, drawing materials for analysis from a wide variety of societies around the world. These materials for analysis come
originally from anthropological fieldwork—that is, from ethnography. In the words of one text:

> The foundation of cultural anthropology is ethnography (Gr. *ethnos*,
> race, peoples and *graphein*, to write). Literally, the word "ethnog-
> raphy" means to write about peoples. As we use the term, it refers
> to the descriptive study of human societies . . . . Ethnography pro-
> vides the building blocks for cultural anthropology [Hoebel 1972,
> pp. 11–12].

Thus, the research you will be doing in connection with the projects in this book is ethnography; and you will be acting as an
ethnographer. The ethnographic material you produce in accordance with the project assignments will, however, constitute
only a portion of the material a complete ethnography includes.
    Anthropological fieldwork, unlike fieldwork in other social
sciences, characteristically involves a long stay among the members of the society being studied in order for the ethnographer
to get a more nearly total view of that society. The usual expec-

tation for the person doing cross-cultural research in a region that has not been systematically studied previously is that he will stay a year or more, so that the way of life of the people can be observed as it varies throughout the different seasons of the year. This is because the ethnographer must get to know a great deal about the total way of life before being able to understand selected portions of it. It does little good to be able to report that a group practices mother-in-law avoidance, parallel-cousin marriage, or any such custom if we cannot say *why* such a custom is practiced or how it fits in with other lifeways of the people. The anthropologist may find, for example, that legends and tales are an important part of the culture history of a primitive people and regulate much of their social and political organization. Folktales and proverbs are often used as teaching devices for training young people in the society's value system. Songs, chants, honorary titles, and curing techniques are often considered private property, which means they are part of the study of economics. It is only when one approaches a culture as a consistent whole that valuable insights can be gained and the meaning and importance of any custom can become apparent.

The lengthy stay necessary for a well-rounded study of the lifeways of a people implies continual interaction with the research subjects and more identification with them. The relationships formed between an ethnographer and the people among whom he works can, and frequently do, develop into lifelong friendships. Obviously, the ethnographer also becomes indebted to those who share with him their possessions, their time, and their knowledge.

The complete ethnography is the result of considerable fieldwork. It tells how members of a society live from the time they are born until they die; the positions they hold at different times in their lives; what they do in these positions and what the society prescribes that they should do; what the systems of belief current in the culture are and what kinds of choices in belief and behavior people have; what ceremonies they may take part in and in what ways; their art and bodily adornments; shelter; ways of making a living; and how this society is related to those of nearby areas.

GETTING TO KNOW A VERY IMPORTANT PERSON: YOURSELF

Obviously, although the work you will be doing on the projects in this book will not result in a complete ethnography, you will learn from firsthand experience many of the things an ethnographer must know. You can also gain this experience while benefitting from the advice and encouragement of an instructor and fellow students; do most of your research in the language you know best; never suffer through being refused a necessary visa; never find it necessary to write while in the throes of a virulent and exotic malady; never force yourself to smile bravely while consuming a succulent reindeer eyeball or a hundred-year-old egg that has been saved especially for you!

While these examples may seem a bit extreme, the fact is that an important part of getting ready to do fieldwork lies in getting to have a better understanding of yourself as a potential research "instrument." Perhaps, like us, you have thought about the anthropologists you know and come to feel that it is no accident that Professor A tends to work in a remote village or tiny island where he or she can know personally every member of the society, while Professor B prefers urban anthropological research in a crowded city, Professor C works among a newly contacted primitive group in a jungle area, and Professor D studies the hippie subculture not far from his home. Few fieldwork projects are chosen solely on the basis of available funding or other practical considerations. Personal factors enter into choices – as indeed they should.

It is not too soon to start thinking about the factors that you yourself would find important in choosing a future research locale. All anthropologists agree that the personal equation is of vital importance. The techniques of ethnographers are, as we have suggested, not so formalized that they can be used without consideration of who is doing the work. There must, eventually, be some consideration of the kinds of people you are drawn to, whether or not you can stand long stories of hunts or long ceremonial chants of ancestries, long reports of arguments or battles. What *you* are interested in is important too, and must play a role in your choices of research sites and subjects – perhaps as you carry out your research for the projects in this course, but surely in any extensive research you plan for the future. We know ethnographers who are sufficiently motivated by their research interests and sufficiently unbothered by particular kinds of field conditions that they undertake, by choice: research involving daily temperatures averaging 40 degrees below zero Fahrenheit; daily temperatures averaging over 110 degrees Fahrenheit, with no shade to be found; cycles of ceremonial activity that may allow little or no sleep for days on end; being repeatedly touched all over as part of becoming acquainted with some primitive peoples; having the hairs of their arms pulled continually while working among people who have never before seen hairy arms; and living in areas where water is so precious that subjects and ethnographer join "the great unwashed" for weeks or months at a time. Clearly, ethnographers who manage quite well under one or the other kind of these circumstances might do far less well under others—and so might you.

Other relevant personal factors are many and varied. They include, of course, the condition of your health and the health of anyone you might take with you, and the necessity to make adequate arrangements for medicine and emergency aid. Knowledge and ability in various technical processes, games, or music and art forms that the local people engage in, or a lively interest in and talent for learning those skills, might also help to influence a choice of location. So, too, might the fact of whether you travel alone or as a member of a group. Advantages of travelling with a family often include easier ability to fit into a community and to be accepted with less suspicion, access to data on more age and sex groups in the community, and, possibly, some division of labor. Advantages of traveling with a team include division of labor, cross-fertilization of ideas, some control of the personal equation, and access to more kinds of data and groups. Disadvantages of doing ethnographic work as a member of a group include the tendency to withdraw and interact too much with one's own group; the larger size of residence required, which may make one less accessible to the local people; the more drastic impact of the ethnographers' presence; and the greater drain on local food and other supplies. It is important to make every effort to avoid being a drain on scarce resources and, at the same time, to plan to buy or trade locally for as many things as possible that the people want to sell, rather than to import supplies. It is far better to make the effort to cooperate in these ways—and, in most cases, people will recognize and appreciate these efforts.

In general, getting to know yourself also includes developing a heightened consciousness of how best to draw upon your personal strengths—social, physical, mental—and how best to compensate for areas of less ability. (We all have them.)

As an ethnographer, the most important single aspect of knowing yourself lies in the ability to divorce yourself from the value judgments that grow out of the fact that you have been raised in a society that has a particular set of standards—moral, ethical, social, sanitary, and so on. *Ethnocentrism*, this business of being "centered" in, and seeing things in terms of, the culture of which one is a product (and that one may somehow think of as superior), is an anthropologist's main bugaboo, something he or she must continually and scrupulously guard against. For ethnocentrism one must try to substitute an attitude of *cultural relativism*, attempting to understand each trait in terms of the total culture. Occasionally, great harm is caused by well-meaning visitors to other societies who do not understand the local lifeways well. Examples include cases where native beers were discouraged or done away with and severe malnutrition resulted; where modern plows were sent in to replace wooden ones and the resulting compacted soils could later be moved only with dynamite; and where gifts of steel axes to replace stone ones resulted in a rather general breakdown of social relations. Even the experienced ethnographer can undergo *culture shock* when he must adapt to some kinds of living patterns; and even he must carefully consider the possible repercussions from his own actions.

We have mentioned that anthropologists are no longer merely the "sociologists for people with no clothes," and that modern ethnographers work in societies that range in complexity from little-contacted and technologically primitive groups to subsections of our own society. As you carry out the research projects suggested in this book, please bear in mind that you have a special challenge to perceive and to report clearly and insightfully upon the cultural patterns of people who are in many respects — especially outwardly — very much like you.

A recent edition of *Notes and Queries on Anthropology* states, "It is important that not even the slightest expression of amazement or disapproval should ever be displayed at the description of ridiculous, impossible or disgusting features in custom, cult, or legend" [Royal Anthropological Institute 1967, p. 32]. At first some of our students greeted this statement itself with amusement and disapproval, but even after short research assignments near their own homes, they have often come to feel differently.

SOME ETHICAL CONSIDERATIONS

Ever since the founding of the first anthropological organizations, there has been much attention to ethics. When the Society for Applied Anthropology was organized, for example, the preparation of its Statement on Ethics was a primary consideration. Some generally agreed upon ethical considerations for planning fieldwork follow.

The fieldworker must present honest statements about the research he is doing and how it will be used. This point cannot be stressed too strongly, for we have known people who placed not only their own research but that of others in grave danger by making false statements. People everywhere are accustomed to "sizing up" others, and, since the ethnographer is constantly a part of the community and under scrutiny because he is interestingly different, he is very likely to be found out.

Another major reason for sticking to true statements about the purposes of one's research is outside the realm of ethics; it is that the more completely and carefully one describes one's purposes to members of the local society, the better they can help with the research. The local people are the ethnographer's teachers about their society. They can make or break his research. We have both had the experience of finding that, once our purposes were explained, many local people turned into excellent amateur ethnographers, anxious to help us know their culture.

One thoroughly conscientious and kindly student of whom we know was interested in the elderly. She hated to state the purpose of her interviews to informants, feeling that, however she stated her purpose, it came out sounding depressingly like, "I want to interview you because you're getting old." She and her roommate decided it would be kindlier to say she was interviewing widows. As a matter of fact, for those women who loved and missed their husbands, it might actually have been harder to think of themselves as widows than as elderly persons. But the real point of using this illustration is that when the student wanted to continue her research on elderly women, no elderly single women, or married women whose husbands were still living, were referred to her because she had defined her interest as "widows." The jig was up when Viet Nam widows in their twenties and thirties were brought to her!

The nature and extent of the explanations one gives depend partly on the sophistication of the group and upon the nature and extent of the contact its members have had with outsiders. Anthropologists may start with an advantage in that people very much want their own anthropologist because nearby groups have had theirs, as Philip Newman [1965] writes of the Gururumba of New Guinea. Or, perhaps, the people have a proud tradition of being kind to strangers and feel they can hear something new from them. On the other hand, one may have a great disadvantage in being mistaken for a government spy, a tax collector, or a "writer" in an area where writers have gotten bad reputations. It is important to find out what kinds of outsiders have bad reputations in order to avoid being taken for one of them.

One of us explained the purpose of her first field research by saying that she had been studying a subject that had to do with the different customs and habits of peoples around the world, and that her university had a requirement that, in addition to learning from books, each person should learn by living and doing research in another society. She had chosen their island because she had heard it was an interesting one to learn about and one about which people should know more. Didn't they agree? They did.

Others explain, for example, that the customs of different peoples vary greatly and that a study of the peoples of the world is being made. If told that the lifeways of nearby peoples have been recorded but that theirs are unknown to much of the rest of the world, most people will react favorably and want to add to the knowledge about their group. Telling about the customs of nearby peoples may, in fact, help in eliciting comments and comparisons. Some recent ethnographers have told their informants that the informants' own descendants would be likely to read their articles or books so it was important that the informants tell everything exactly correctly for the sake of their own offspring [Royal Anthropological Institute 1967, p. 33].

A second major kind of ethical consideration for the fieldworker is his responsibility for making clear as soon and as definitely as possible what he can and cannot do for the members of the society in which he is working. He might need, for example, to make it clear that he is a student, working with very limited funds, and not the wealthy and indolent traveller he may appear to be, or that he cannot get jobs and entry permits for everyone who would like to migrate to his home country.

A third kind of ethical consideration lies in the area which recent United States publications call "Protection of the Individual as a Research Subject." This includes the ethnographer's duty to make and to honor promises of maintaining the anonymity of informants, to present the material as honestly and completely as possible but to bear in mind that the informants or their children and neighbors may read the ethnography someday. It also includes the idea that an ethnographer owes his hosts a great debt for their cooperation and must be careful to repay it in part by, for example, not reporting on them so that punitive agencies can take action against them. Maintaining the anonymity of informants includes not only cases where names must be "changed to protect the innocent," but also the responsibility for not using materials that could be traced to an informant by local people and used to his or her detriment.

In some cases where the ethnographer easily can be associated with a specific place, or an adequate description of the research locus and the culture would make it impossible to preserve the anonymity of the population or of people within it, other ethical arrangements may have to be made. For example, in a recent life-history project in a literate society, we found it necessary to tell our informants, from the beginning, that it would, for a variety of reasons, be impossible and undesirable to hide their identity. We told them—at the risk of losing "juicy tidbits"—that we would use their real names and perhaps even their photographs. When the life histories had been transcribed, each subject was asked to sign a statement that his was a true transcription of his own words and that he approved its publication with a group of life histories.

"Protection of the Individual as a Research Subject" includes many things, and is an ongoing problem. When you leave an area (and afterward when you have written about it), your relations with the people should be such that you would be welcome to return there and so would any other visiting scientist.

The final major ethical matter that we feel should be mentioned is the need to be sure of what a sponsoring agency expects from you when you accept its support, and to be sure that this does not include, for example, quasi-spy roles.

BEFORE GOING TO THE FIELD

An anthropologist goes to another society, or even to a different portion of his own national society, with a definite theoretical frame of reference, often one to which he has devoted years of formal study. Characteristically, also, the area to which he goes is part of a region in which he has special training and with whose affairs he tries to keep up to date. It almost goes without saying that for any of your course projects that involve communities or groups with which you are not already quite familiar, it would be wise if you began as soon as possible to familiarize yourself with as many details as possible of the area where you want to work, and to meet some of the people whom you will want as future research subjects. You might want to begin by reading their newspapers and any existing chamber of commerce or tourism literature, attending public performances and lectures, church socials, sporting events, and so on. Some members of communities close to university or college campuses may be weary of being research subjects, hence special consideration and tact might be required in these areas.

Before leaving for the field and immediately after arrival, the ethnographer must be sure to secure permissions and clear his project with the proper government bureaus and officials. Visas for some areas take many months to secure, so their procurement may have to begin early. Some countries require, either as a supplement to a visa or as a precondition for its issuance, a certificate or letter from one's local police department, attesting to a lack of criminal status. Even where that is not specifically required, it may often be exceedingly useful. One of the things about which many governments or their officials like to be assured is that incoming people have sufficient funds and will not become public charges. It is often good to ask university officials to include such a pledge when they write letters of introduction on behalf of the ethnographer. While comparable arrangements in advance are, of course, not necessary for your projects in this course, please begin early to consider what arrangements you should make with officials and with the heads of any organizations with which you will be working.

Any equipment of foreign make that one plans to take into the field should be registered with one's local customs officials before departure in order to avoid having to pay duty on it when returning home. This registration can also be done in advance in many areas, which often saves time and avoids frantic rushing around when one is at an international airport or dock departing for overseas. It is also wise to check the customs regulations of the host country and be guided by their provisions. For a few countries, it would be wise to take to the field letters addressed to the local officials abroad from officials at a university or sponsoring agency attesting to the validity of the research to be undertaken and the legitimate need for the specific equipment and supplies. In your research for this course, although visas and regulations about importing goods through customs will be no problem, you might be well advised to check on what equipment and supplies you can and cannot "import." For example, many churches forbid the taking of flash photographs during weddings, baptisms, and other services.

The World Health Organization and other agencies provide useful information about health conditions around the world. Publications containing this information can often be obtained from a good travel agent or from the governmental agency where passports are procured. It would also be good to supplement this information with advice from anyone who has recently worked and lived nearby and knows the conditions of your field site as well. This applies not only to advice about shots and medicines to take along but also to vitamins and diet supplements. For anyone who will be moving around a great deal or dealing with rough terrain (domestic or foreign), a tetanus shot is usually advisable, although tetanus boosters for those who have had initial inoculations are no longer given as frequently as they once were. These are all matters that should be talked over with a doctor during a prefieldwork checkup. Sometimes pharmaceutical companies will provide free samples of medication to scientists about to conduct field research. Occasionally, if the fieldwork locus has not been thoroughly explored for their purposes, a pharmaceutical company may give small grants to fieldworkers in exchange for soil samples or properly prepared botanical specimens that will indicate to the company whether or not the site is of potential value for the growth of medicinal plants.

Checking transportation schedules and arrangements well in advance often pays, not only from the point of view of catching instead of missing the monthly steamer, or the weekly plane, or sloop, but also because added familiarity with transport systems often brings a bonus in the form of better or less expensive service. For example, if arrangements are made in advance, it is sometimes possible to take with you on the same plane those things you planned to send as "air freight." By asking that they be taken "air freight" on the same plane, one may be able to avoid all the bother and expense involved with special pick-up and delivery and separate processing through customs, as well as the huge bill that would result if such things were carried with regular luggage and billed as "excess baggage." For the immediate purposes of your projects for this course, transportation may not be a major problem, but we mention it as part of giving you a check list.

GETTING TO KNOW AND WORK WITH OTHERS

This book has been written with the idea "you, too, can do good fieldwork" as a general theme; we find that the aspect of fieldwork about which our students are most concerned (and we ourselves have been, also) is the matter of whether or not they can achieve and maintain rapport with the people among whom they work. As one anthropologist has put it, "The only information of value is that which people give freely. People do not speak freely unless they feel at home with the interviewer." Feeling at home with the interviewer is obviously related to his or her feeling at home with the people in question. Although the topics of beginning fieldwork and of interviewing an informant could form part of this introductory section, because of their importance we have made these topics the subjects of separate chapters. Please refer to Projects 1 and 4 for detailed discussion of these subjects.

THREE BASIC PRINCIPLES TO FOLLOW

There are many rules that could be set up for fieldwork. You will find a good many suggestions throughout this book, but we have chosen to emphasize just three things we believe are of great importance for the collection of field notes. We urge you to keep them in mind as you carry out each project.

1. *Label your work carefully.* Each and every field note should be carefully labeled with the date on which the notation was made, a page number, and, if possible, a topic heading. A typewriter transcription of field notes taken at an earlier date should be labeled with both the date on which the notes were first taken and the date of transcription. *Always make carbon copies of any typewritten notes* and store the carbon copies for safekeeping, somewhere away from the originals.

2. *Make extensive, detailed notes.* This is an idea of potential usefulness in conjunction with your projects for this course, but will become vital for any extended fieldwork. We want to underscore it for several reasons. Presumably, most people who take courses in anthropological fieldwork methods do so because they are interested in their fellow humans. Such people may feel that they have been keen observers for a long while and have such excellent memories that they do not need to rely on extensive note-taking. We urge you not to adopt this attitude. For one thing, a good collection of field notes can be of value for decades, and no one can remember perfectly all the myriad fine-grain details of a lengthy period of fieldwork and their exact time sequence. Secondly, an unexpected event in the future might make it essential to reexamine the happenings that led up to the event. Thirdly, an extensive collection of field materials can be mined again and again, now for

details on one subject, now for details on another. Verbatim quotations, or, failing that, close paraphrases of an informant's words, are especially valuable and help establish the proper feeling tone. It is an excellent idea to include in your field notes some indications of the conditions under which you were making the notes and — preferably in some special notational system that could not be read by the local people — thoughts such as "I have the feeling he is hiding something here," or "Remember to check this out with a specialist."

3. *Check up on yourself.* We have found checks of various kinds to be of value, both those in such compilations as *Notes and Queries, Outline of Cultural Materials, Field Guide to the Ethnological Study of Child Life,* and so on, and those that we ourselves have written in the field. Our suggestions throughout the book are merely starters. We hope you will use them as building blocks; but we suggest that, as often as possible, you review your work of the day, asking yourself what questions are suggested by the information you have recently uncovered, what avenues of approach you have not tried, which of the things that you know perfectly well to ask and to do you have let slip.

SELECTED ANNOTATED BIBLIOGRAPHY

Hilger, Sr. M. Inez
   Field Guide to the Ethnological Study of Child Life. Human Relations Area Files, 1966.
Hoebel, E. Adamson
   Anthropology: The Study of Man. McGraw-Hill, 4th ed., 1972. One of the more popular general introductory texts.
Kroeber, A. L., ed.
   Anthropology Today: An Encyclopedic Inventory. University of Chicago Press, 1953. An important compilation, though now 20 years old.
Maranda, Pierre
   Introduction to Anthropology: A Self-Guide. Prentice-Hall, 1972.
Murdock, G. P., et al., eds.
   Outline of Cultural Materials. Human Relations Area Files, 4th rev. ed., 1971. A handy checklist for fieldwork.
Newman, Philip
   Knowing the Gururumba. Holt, Rinehart and Winston, 1965. A short ethnography which contains very good material on beginning fieldwork.

Royal Anthropological Institute of Great Britain and Ireland
Notes and Queries on Anthropology. London: Routledge and Kegan Paul,
6th ed., 1967. The best-known single anthropological field manual.
Spradley, James P., and David W. McCurdy
The Cultural Experience: Ethnography in Complex Society. Science Research
Associates, 1972.
Tylor, Edward B.
*Primitive Culture: Researches into the Development of Mythology, Philosophy,
Religion, Language, Art and Custom.* London: Murray, 1871. A classic – but
mentioned here simply because of the quoted definitions of culture.

PROJECT ONE

BEGINNING FIELDWORK

INTRODUCTION

One anthropologist began his book by asking, rather plaintively, who ever reads introductions anyway. We hope the answer is that you do, for the one in this book contains some information which may be of help in connection with the first project and many of your future research projects as well. As we suggested in that introduction, if you are typical of most of the people we have known who were contemplating their first anthropological fieldwork, you are especially concerned about the initial stages of your fieldwork, and, in particular, about achieving rapport with those among whom you will work. Because these feelings are so common, one author entitles the initial chapter of her book on fieldwork "The First and Most Uncomfortable Stage," and speaks of the beginning fieldworker as living in a social limbo, trying to behave as if he belongs and as if he knows what he is doing [Wax 1971, p. 19].

Obviously, however, since such a high proportion of all anthropologists think of their periods in the field as the most rewarding and exciting periods of their careers, despite such problems as having to undergo some initial discomfort, anyone seriously thinking of anthropology as a career should persevere in learning about fieldwork. Fortunately, students now have an opportunity to benefit from the experience of others, experience that is finally being written about more clearly and candidly, and in greater detail. Suggestions gleaned from the experience of many people are woven into each project in this book, those in this chapter emphasizing the initial phases of fieldwork.

Definite rules for making contact with members of other societies cannot be laid down. The attitudes of members of the host society will depend in large measure upon the contacts the people in question have had with outsiders; since, in some instances, those contacts have been very unfortunate, the ethnographer must take this into consideration, and adjust his behavior accordingly.

Apart from the possibility of encountering extreme shyness or aggressive hostility, the ethnographer may be faced with any of a large range of attitudes requiring sensitivity, patience, and tact. In areas where other social scientists have previously worked and no benefits to the local people have resulted, the ethnographer may have to cope with extreme apathy and a feeling of superiority toward both him and the items of material culture he brings with him. Local people who are smotheringly attentive because they want to exact favors or associate themselves with outsiders can be particularly embarassing to the ethnographer who has not yet established himself locally.

One general necessity upon arrival is to contact the local officials or headmen with whom the research has to be cleared. Presumably these are among the people with whom the ethnographer has already been in correspondence, if they are literate. The nature of the arrangements an ethnographer can make is often determined in large measure by the host group itself. The well-known British anthropologist E. E. Evans-Pritchard has remarked in connection with two of his fieldwork experiences in Africa that the two groups structured their relationships to him in completely different ways. The Azande would not allow him to live as one of them, but compelled him to live outside the village, and treated him as a superior. The Nuer, on the other hand, compelled him to live right among them and as an equal.

A first consideration upon arrival in the field is to establish a base of operations. Basically, for fieldwork of longer duration than any you will be carrying out for the projects in this course, this means a household, although a vantage point in a sidewalk café, or some comparable locus in other fieldwork situations, may also become established as a rather regular headquarters, either until permanent household arrangements have been made or as a supplement to them. You may also want to establish a part-time base of operations if you will be doing much of your research for this course in one area. Sites in the midst of the action of the community where observation is easier are ideal. Often the local people will be of help in this regard. Housing or research loci that are as much like the other housing of the community as possible will help to encourage the people to feel free to visit and, sometimes, to establish more relaxed neighborly relations in general. Maintaining a household in the field — especially where there is very little house to hold — can be very helpful in combating ethnocentric tendencies on the part of the ethnographer, especially where he or she is the one doing the housekeeping and dealing on a day-to-day basis with the many time-consuming and frustrating problems it can entail.

There are a great many aspects of establishing oneself in the field situation about which one can look to the local people for guidance. This may sound like such an obvious statement as to be unnecessary, but the fact is that many of us initially fail to profit from the clues that the local culture provides. As an example, we might cite the fact that in many areas "unattached" women who move freely about the community or live alone in guest houses are virtually unknown and may, therefore, be perceived as "loose" women or aberrent individuals. Female ethnographers do have some specific problems with which to deal, as most of them are acutely aware. We know one attractive female ethnographer who took her six-foot-three son along as "chaperone" on her second trip to a particular area. But six-foot sons are not standard operating equipment for most women, and the local culture may provide solutions. For example, in many societies it is the custom to have youngsters spend the evening and the night with those who would otherwise be alone. This custom can often be put into effect for the ethnographer very easily, sometimes to the obvious pleasure — even relief — of the local people, who are pleased to find ethnographers of either sex behaving in ways to which they themselves are accustomed.

We suggested above that the ethnographer must, at least to some extent, accept and work within the social position the local people are willing to give him. On the other hand, he must proceed with considerable caution in establishing relationships when first in the field in order to avoid being associated in people's minds with undesirables. Unfortunately, sometimes those who make themselves most available do so because their fellow citizens find them less desirable. Nor should the ethnographer prejudice his reception by associating at first with a group considered pariahs by a group that he wishes to investigate later — for example, associating a great deal with untouchables and then trying to move to a very high-caste group would cause problems in India.

The preceding paragraph obviously suggests many potential problems. Some of these can be taken care of, or considerably lessened, in connection with an all-important matter we have stressed before—carefully describing the purposes of one's work. We mentioned in the Introduction that carefully describing one's purposes helps people to understand and cooperate with the work. It can also help them to understand why the ethnographer wants and needs to work with all of the kinds of people who make up the society, not solely with the most prestigious, the cleanest, or those with the most education. Since getting to know people is not a one-way street, and the personal factors cannot all be controlled, the ethnographer can make his or her interests explicit and, in exchanging information with people, can let them know about his or her own background, family, and interests. With time and the establishment of understandings, local people may come to shield the ethnographer insightfully from those who would be potential nuisances. This assistance, however, is something to be watched very carefully lest problems inadvertently be created. A person supposedly acting on behalf of the ethnographer may unconsciously offend people or unknowingly turn away people the ethnographer wants very much to see.

Every ethnographer in the field, however great his experience, is still very much the learner, the members of the host society, the teachers. Every culture has its own conventions, its rules of conduct and etiquette. These, and the common forms of greeting, should be learned as quickly as possible. In some areas where we have worked, for example, the common greeting is that of "doing your hand" (waving) to passersby. Those visitors who do it regularly are seen as friendly and interested in the local people. In order to be certain to do the things that please people and not blunder into doing things that are displeasing or offensive, it is best to make your desire to learn and your good intentions clear at the outset. It is likely that any unwitting mistakes will then be overlooked or regarded as ignorance on the part of a stranger.

In general, it is wise to move slowly at first. Care is needed because the areas that are sensitive topics for conversation may differ greatly from place to place. In some areas one must be guarded in discussing corruption, in others one must avoid talking about physiology and prostitution, and in other places secret cults or religious beliefs outside the formalized church are the sensitive topics. Only after one has learned the "touchy" points of a culture can one make good judgments about what questions to ask and when to ask them, when to take pictures, and when to tape record. It is important to realize that *your* touchy areas may not be those of the local people. Perhaps public opinion will force you to move in where you would not have. When a death occurred for the first time in the community where one of us was studying, the ethnographer's first inclination was to observe the funeral procession and services quietly and inconspicuously, not intruding upon the family "in their hour of sorrow." Local people quickly let it be known that anyone with a camera should not be at the back of a crowd and urged, even pushed, ethnographer and camera to the most central (and conspicuous) place because, they said, obviously overseas relatives would like photographs of the deceased and of the large crowd that had turned out to honor her!

An interest in language, technical processes, music, art, photography, or string figures is not likely to be regarded with suspicion, and may often prove to be a better beginning for anthropological work than direct questioning. Someone who can take an interest in crafts or games, and can perhaps contribute something to them, will always have an advantage. A friend of ours who has the ability to turn his handkerchief into a fascinating jumping frog, a lazy turtle, or a hopping rabbit was quietly showing his creatures to a group of children in a Mexican mountain village when he found that they captivated young and old alike, and were wonderful "ice breakers." While the ethnographer will be anxious to join people in their activities and perhaps to make contributions himself, he should not expect to have his creations admired more than the local products. It is usually wise to assume the attitude of a learner as often as possible, rather than that of a teacher, especially since that will consistently remind people that you are anxious to be taught.

In the first days in the field, while one is slowly becoming acquainted, anthropologists have found it good to begin with such things as mapping the community, assigning numbers to households and fields, and so on, so that ownership and working of the land, and membership in the household can later be made clear and explicit with number designations. General observations can also be begun, of course, starting with things like who goes to the well or standpipe with whom, who chats with whom, who visits whom, who goes to collect pension checks with whom, gestures, and identification of people within the group. It is also good to begin to become familiar with material objects such as clothing, houses, and implements, and their construction patterns. Since the anthropologist in the field depends for so much of his information upon the things he sees, he must be observant and also able to organize and utilize his observations. All such observations suggest topics for later questions and interviews, as well as serving to verify interview data. In societies that possess the art of writing or of making other kinds of records, there may be scriptures; historical documents such as wills, deeds, or marriage records; inscriptions on stone, metal, or wood, and so on, that are sufficiently uncontroversial or public to be good subjects for early copying and study.

Much can, of course, be learned from early pure observation; but when tied in with participation and interviewing, observation becomes more valuable. In his work with his informants, the ethnographer uses two kinds of interviews, nondirective and directive. Nondirective interviewing involves asking the informant to discuss a general area of culture. Typical questions might be, "Please tell me about your life as a child," or "Please tell me more about _____." The nondirective interview is used frequently in the early phases of research, since it allows the informant to talk freely about things that interest him and seem important to him. This can be useful in bringing to light many things the anthropologist might overlook because of the lack of an equivalent situation in his own culture, and in giving him some insights into the perspectives of the local people. The anthropologist must be willing to take into consideration all sorts of information of importance to the lives of the people, including that which contradicts his pet theories or original formulations.

Nondirective questioning is useful throughout fieldwork; and, with the passage of time, more directive interviewing can be done. Directive interviewing means that the ethnographer, instead of suggesting broad areas for general coverage, uses more narrowly focused questions, zeroing in on specific things. (Being "directive," of course, does not involve implying answers to one's questions!)

In societies where questionnaires and standardized interviews can be used, the information they provide can be valuable for getting facts quickly, for checking on yourself, and, importantly, for getting information that is comparable from case to case. Any framing and use of questionnaires should, however, be done only when the ethnographer has already learned something about the culture and after a pretest. That is, before the questionnaire is administered to subjects, it should be tested by asking members of the local community to take the test and/or to make sure that the wording and the concepts can be completely understood by the people to be questioned, and that the questions are relevant, fair, and inoffensive. It is also sometimes rewarding to find out what questions some local people would suggest adding to the questionnaire.

Whether as part of an unstructured interview or in a questionnaire, the "hypothetical situation" can often be used to good advantage. The well-known scholar in Afro-American cultures Melville Herskovits was one of those who strongly advocated the technique for getting information about practices or traditions without referring to specific people or events. It is, for example, more diplomatic to ask, "What would happen if a boy were caught stealing apples?" than to say, "I understand your nephew was caught stealing fruit. What will happen to him?" Herskovits and others have shown that by using hypothetical situations the ethnographer can free his informant to speak about happenings and the patterning of events in ways he would not feel able to if he were talking about specific, real individuals.

As we have suggested, choices about which of the many kinds of questioning to use, the wording of questions, and when and of whom to ask them can usually all be handled best when the ethnographer has accumulated knowledge and experience of the culture. The fieldworker characteristically moves gradually from pure observation to more participant observation, from nondirective to more directive questions. When the ethnographer has established some of the kinds of relationships that will enable him to do his fieldwork, he can move out gradually to other types of exploration. Rosalie Wax has described this stage in the development of a fieldworker so effectively that we can do no better than to quote her:

> Once the fieldworker has managed to establish some reciprocal relationships with his hosts, he will find, sometimes very suddenly, that his anxieties and his feelings of incompetence and stupidity have decreased to a marked degree and that he is able to work on a new and very encouraging level of competence. Indeed, the process of involvement is circular and cumulative. The less anxious a fieldworker is, the better he works, and, as he becomes aware that he is doing good work, he becomes less anxious. Usually the essential factor in this transformation is the assistance and support—the reciprocal social response—given him by some of his hosts. It is in their company that he begins to do the kind of "participation and observation" that enables him to "understand" what is going on about him at his own speed and at his own level of competence. It is his hosts who will let him know when he behaves stupidly or offensively, and will reassure him when he thinks he has made some gross blunder. It is they who will help him meet the people who can assist

him in his work, and it is they who will tell him when his life is in danger and when it is not. As this process continues, the fieldworker often becomes quite skillful and self-confident in his own right. He no longer lies awake at night tormenting himself over the question of whether or not he hurt this or that person's feelings or overlooked some particular opportunity. He finds himself doing with assurance many things over which, previously, he hesitated and worried for days. He learns how to behave in the presence of old people, young women, children, and infants. He begins to learn how to accept obligations and how to repay them, when to ask questions and when to keep his mouth shut—in short, how to stay out of the most obvious kinds of trouble. Indeed, in the literal, ancient, and comforting sense of the phrase, he now begins "to know what he is doing" [1971, p. 20].*

Between the lines of Dr. Wax's words, and in some of our own words, you have probably realized that someone who cannot abide feeling awkward or out of place, who feels crushed whenever he makes a mistake or when anyone laughs at his ineptness, is bound to have a particularly hard time as a fieldworker. It is a basic fact that anyone conducting ethnographic research in a culture or subculture that is not one in which he was raised *is* a "ludicrous tenderfoot" who knows a lot less about what he is doing in some respects than a small native child, and that making fun of inept behavior has been a corrective measure through long periods of man's history. It is precisely because all of the people whose writings on fieldwork we mention in this book have had similar humbling experiences on the way to becoming more seasoned ethnographers that we and they want to pass suggestions along, with a sense of sharing.

There is one thing that Dr. Wax stresses about which we, too, are willing to be rather hard-nosed. She states [p. 47] that "the most egregious error that a fieldworker can commit" is to assume he can win the immediate regard of the people among whom he works by telling them he wants to become one of them, or by implying that the fact they tolerate his presence means he *is* one of them. She points out that people seldom resent the person who wants to learn their ways or even to act as they do— imitation being the sincerest form of flattery—so long as the fieldworker makes it clear that he knows he is playing a part and that any newly acquired skills do not entitle him to privileges that they are not willing to offer him. Nevertheless:

> What people do resent—sometimes very deeply—is the amateurish
> notion that the acquisition of a few tricks or a sentimental statement
> about universal brotherhood will, almost automatically, turn a
> clumsy and ignorant outsider into an experienced, hardened,
> expert, or sacred person like themselves [Wax, p. 49].*

This does not mean that devotion to sentiments of brotherhood
and high levels of motivation to work considerately and conscien-
tiously are not appreciated by other anthropologists, or by the
people being studied. It does mean that the person will be
judged much more on the basis of how he lives his life in the
community and how he treats those around him than upon anything he says about his intentions. Although the ethnographer
may become the close and trusted friend of those among whom
he works, he is different from them in various ways and will
never become completely an insider, truly a part of the culture
he is studying. It is usually best if he maintains his identity as a
deeply interested, tolerant, respectful, and respectable member
of another society. Emphatically, being a participant observer
does not add up to "going native."

As you begin to contemplate the various projects for this
course, please note that the first two projects will rely almost
completely upon keen observation, and that the next two projects will each require you to work with only one informant. Thus,
rapport-building on a wider scale will not come until the later
projects. Please concentrate at first, then, on striving to open
"new" eyes on life around you. Perhaps you have spent your
whole life thus far in a community very like those in which you
will conduct your research for the course, or even in the very
same community. There is a special challenge to working among
people whom you have known rather well (or thought you did),
and who may even be very like you in outward appearances.
Whether or not you experience a mild form of what anthropologists call "culture shock," (the shock resulting from being confronted with an unfamiliar way of life whose clues elude you),
try to look at the situation as if you were a visiting foreigner—or
even a man from Mars. Take nothing for granted; observe as
sharply and objectively as you can. Try to develop the habit of
being as aware as possible of what goes on around you at all
times, and strive for new insights on old, familiar subjects as well
as new ones.

THE PROJECT

There are, of course, a great many things that would make interesting research subjects for an initial excursion into "the field." We have chosen a topic that our students find challenging, and that has not been so extensively explored that you yourselves may not chart some new waters. Our topic is *proxemics*.

We know that our spoken and written language is our most important medium of communication. We are also aware that we can communicate a good deal by the way we shrug our shoulders, stick out our tongues, or give dirty looks. But it is only in the last fifteen years or so that Edward T. Hall and some of his associates have shown us clearly that "space speaks" and "time talks."

"Proxemics" is the term Hall uses in connection with man's perception and use of space—that is, he studies the relative proximity of people to one another in various situations and in various societies. He shows that how people handle space in connection with their human interactions can silently tell us a great deal, can "speak volumes." Since each society of the world has different patterns of space use, we can distort intercultural communication easily and, by our use of space, give messages we do not intend. For example, the standard distances that people keep between them in public conversation in some societies—and it is important to realize that they are quite standardized distances—are far smaller than the distance observed in our society. When people from such societies come equally close to converse with Americans, they intrude upon the space we consider "personal," and we may unconsciously feel threatened and move away a little. The words of our diplomats may be carefully phrased; and, at the same time, we may be becoming "ugly Americans" because of the messages we send by how we use space. Like the birds often so evenly spaced on a telephone wire, each of us may, depending upon the situation, want an envelope of personal space around himself. The size of that envelope depends very much upon the way that space use was patterned in the particular culture or subculture in which each of us was raised.

Hall points out [1955, p. 4] that in the United States "we have strong feelings about touching and being crowded; in a streetcar, bus or elevator we draw ourselves in. Toward a person who relaxes and lets himself come into full contact with others in a crowded place we usually feel reactions that could not be printed on this page." People tell children not to sit so close or breathe "down their necks." In conversation a United States male brought up in the northeast stands eighteen to twenty inches away when talking face-to-face with a man he does not know very well; and when talking to a woman under similar circumstances he adds four inches. A distance of only eight to thirteen inches between males, which Hall finds the only comfortable conversational distance in many parts of Latin America and the Middle East, would, in the United States, be considered either very aggressive or, perhaps, almost sexual. Hall portrays United States businessmen in Latin America as trying to maintain their preferred distances by barricading themselves behind tables, desks and typewriters, only to have visitors circle around or jump over the barriers in order to establish conversational distances that will be comfortable for them. Neither party is aware of just what is wrong when distance is not right; but both have feelings of discomfort and anxiety, both take offense without knowing why. On one occasion, Hall saw two men, one a Latin American and one a North American, begin a conversation at one end of a forty-foot hall and end it at the other, the North American having backed the whole way down the hall trying to establish a comfortable distance between himself and the Latin American, who continually advanced, trying to establish his own comfortable distance for conversation.

How people use space can communicate in much the same way as does tone of voice. It can be, like language, "formal or informal, warm or cold, public or private, masculine or feminine, and indicative of high or low status" [Hall 1960, p. 45]. Patterns of space use vary from nation to nation; and the same pattern can give very different messages in different parts of the world. Hall found, for example, that a Chinese man whom he interviewed seemed quite tongue-tied when he spoke with him face to face or at an angle but became talkative when Hall found out he was accustomed to side-by-side placement of furniture and placed himself appropriately.

People in every society grow up learning to move through space and interact with others in the patterned ways that their respective societies consider appropriate and that are related to the society's own lifestyle, patterns of architectural design, furniture placement, and so on. In Japan, for example, the walls are movable and can be opened and closed as the day's activities or people's moods change. The walls screen visually, but with only paper walls the acoustic "screening" is minimal. Japanese tend to focus on arranging the furniture in the center of a room, while in the United States we tend to arrange furniture around the walls, leaving the center of the room empty. Even knowing that the Japanese concentrate on the arrangement of centers, it strikes Americans as amazing that the Japanese give names to intersections, but not to streets. Houses on the streets are numbered in the order that they are built, so that finding a particular house may be quite difficult for visitors. United States occupation forces in Tokyo named a few main routes, and it will be interesting to see how long the names remain.

One thing that has been found to be generally true is that the vast majority of people in every society are not aware of how they are using space. In response to questions, they cannot say precisely why they feel uneasy or pressed in some situations, more comfortable in others. Obviously, we do not have to adjust our lives completely to conform to the space-use patterns of those with whom we are interacting. As Hall suggests, we are expected to be different; but we can learn to communicate better with others by being sensitive to the unwritten patterns to which they are accustomed. To be aware that there are pitfalls in cross-cultural relations on the basis of differences in space use is a big step forward.

Clashes between people who employ different systems of space use are not limited to international relations. Several social scientists, including Hall, report that while the members of many of the diverse groups that make up United States society may sound basically alike and look alike, beneath the surface there lie many unformulated differences in the structuring of time, space, and relationships [Hall 1969, p. x]. Commenting upon some of Hall's work, Weston LaBarre [1968] makes some interesting suggestions regarding ways in which space use may be seen to differ regionally in the United States and to have a sex component, an age component, and probably a status component as well.

The first assignment is to design and carry out an experiment in some aspect of how our society or some subsociety uses space. For example, you might focus upon how people use the tables in a library reading room. How is the use of tables and chairs different if the people know one another and/or come in together and converse at the table from cases where they appear not to know one another? Alternatively, you might want to examine how people arrange themselves on busses or trains, at clinics, or in a waiting room. Please note that this may require more than one observation period, or a fairly long period in one place, to get the detailed notes you will require.

One thing you might find useful to explore is the extent to which the spaces you study and the furniture within them tend to keep people apart or to draw them together. Following studies by a physician named Osmond, Hall [1969, p. 108] speaks of such areas as railway waiting rooms as "sociofugal" (those that keep people apart) and some, like the tables at a French sidewalk café, as "sociopetal" (those that tend to bring people together). Sociofugal space is not necessarily bad, nor sociopetal space good; but an understanding of the concepts has led to insights into such matters as how to discourage crowding and clogging spaces that need to be kept free, how to encourage interaction between patients in nursing homes, and so on. Robert Sommer [cited in Hall 1963, p. 435], in a study on the effect of spatial arrangements on human interaction, rearranged the furniture in a model ward of a hospital where the patients had been apathetic despite bright and cheerful surroundings. "As a result of these rearrangements, the number of conversations doubled, and intake of information through reading tripled." Does your research suggest any ideas as to how changes in space use might bring about better human interaction or fewer misunderstandings?

This project in proxemics was chosen as the focus of a beginning chapter partly because it can be carried out purely on the basis of observation and can provide information of immediate practical value about the space use, interaction patterns, and so on, of the group being studied. Ideally, all of us should also use this kind of concept in an ongoing way, both in observing and understanding patterns of space use and in learning to be sensitive and responsive to such factors ourselves.

SELECTED ANNOTATED BIBLIOGRAPHY

Fried, Morton H.
    The Study of Anthropology. Crowell, 1972. A helpful book for any anthro-
    pology student, giving some attention to fieldwork but also guidance and
    useful insights on many subjects.
Hall, Edward T., Jr.
    "The Anthropology of Manners." *Scientific American*, 1955, 4:84–90.
Hall, Edward T., Jr.
    The Silent Language. Doubleday, 1959.
Hall, Edward T., Jr.
    "The Language of Space." *Landscape: Magazine of Human Geography*, 1960,
    1:41–45.
Hall, Edward T., Jr.
    "Proxemics: The Study of Man's Spatial Relations." In Iago Galdston, ed.,
    Man's Image in Medicine and Anthropology. International Universities Press,
    1963.
Hall, Edward T., Jr.
    "Silent Assumptions in Social Communication." In David McK. Rioch and
    Edwin A. Weinstein, eds., *Disorders of Communication*, 1964. Proceedings of
    the Association for Research in Nervous and Mental Disease, XLII (Decem-
    ber 7 and 8, 1962).
Hall, Edward T., Jr.
    "Proxemics." *Current Anthropology*, 1968, 9(2–3):83–95.
Hall, Edward T., Jr.
    The Hidden Dimension. Doubleday, 1969.
Hall, Edward T., Jr., and William Foote White

"Intercultural Communication: A Guide to Men of Action." *Human Organization*, 1960, 1:5–12. All of these references to Hall's work are results of his extensive research on how people use time and space.

Wax, Rosalie H.

Doing Fieldwork: Warnings and Advice. University of Chicago Press, 1971. An engaging and helpful book that covers the author's own field experience and the lessons she learned.

PROJECT TWO

MAKING MAPS

INTRODUCTION

Mapping is essentially a way of organizing and setting down observations. The information recorded will be of importance throughout the research, and later can be used in connection with a variety of matters such as genealogical and census data. For the anthropologist, whether he is an ethnographer or an archaeologist, an important consideration behind map making will always be the ties between physical space and social relationships. The cartographic technique, in a sense, enables one to rise above the immediate range of vision and consider the features and relationships of larger areas, whether the view is obstructed by a natural jungle or a "concrete jungle."

As we noted in the first project, an activity characteristically beginning early in the anthropologist's fieldwork is "getting the lay of the land." The fieldworker constructs a village or regional map, showing housing, agricultural land, fishing or hunting territories, important water resources, and whatever else his problem and research design make it important for him to know. If plots of land are owned or controlled by families, he also can begin to note such boundaries or divisions.

Map making is an excellent device for building rapport during the period when the researcher is most likely to be uncomfortable in a new field situation. It gives him a readily understandable reason for establishing contacts with people. During the construction of the maps and later, the maps help greatly by reminding informants and researcher alike of additional information that should be recorded. Please note that we suggested earlier that almost any topic can turn out to be a sensitive one in at least some parts of the world. Map making is no exception. Therefore, it is wise to find out about and benefit from the experience of others who have done mapping in the area. Here again, it is essential to inform people of the purposes of your work, so that you will be less likely to be thought a government spy or tax assessor.

Work with local people from the beginning of your mapping project, so as to benefit from their insights about what is useful and what is culturally significant in their area. Most people know their habitats intimately, especially if their livelihood depends rather directly on the land, which, of course, changes through the seasons. Rather than marking off an area with a superimposed grid system, or sticking strictly to the ideas given by government maps and data sheets, the fieldworker should be guided by local people in learning the culturally significant boundaries. Anthropologists in the Philippines and in the mountains of New Guinea find that the people themselves recognize far more types of soil and plants in their regions than are reported by formal survey. These "native categories" of soils and plants may also be significant in determining the location of fields and house plots. Many societies have concepts of land ownership and land usage that do not conform to the systems imposed by their governments. It is also a good idea to note local names for features of the landscape and to use them in eliciting data.

A common request in our society is, "Let's get down to brass tacks," an expression that comes from the custom of driving tacks into a sales counter for use in measuring lengths of dry goods. Our admonition, "Mind your p's and q's' derives from the old tavernkeepers' warning to customers that they should be mindful of the number of pints and quarts already charged to their accounts. People everywhere choose units of measurement that have meaning in their daily lives; and all of these may provide clues for the researcher. Conklin has shown, for example, that among some Philippine peoples walking distances are stated in terms of the number of chews of betel nut one would consume on the way.

Cartographers sometimes speak of their art as a "universal language," practiced by people everywhere to at least some degree. Many fieldworkers personally experience the fact that the making of maps antedates the art of writing in the societies they study. For the members of preliterate societies, knowledge of directions, distances, and landmarks can be a life-or-death matter. Devices constructed by some early Pacific islanders with frameworks of reed or the midribs of palm leaves proved to be ingenious navigation charts for sailing between islands, each of which was represented by a shell attached to the frame. Eskimo wooden pocketpieces whittled in the shapes of portions of the Alaskan coastline have long been admired for their accuracy.

No one knows, of course, who made the very first map. The one that is believed to be the oldest in existence is a tiny clay tablet found by Harvard researchers in the ruined city of Ga Sur, 200 miles from the ancient city of Babylon. Like many maps down through history, it was probably used to show landholding. Such landholding maps are called cadastral maps—their main use is for the purpose of assessing taxes. Although cadastral maps may exist for the area in which an anthropologist is working, they are one type of map that he may find he cannot ethically accept if officials expect in return genealogical or other private data that could be used to the detriment of his informants.

FIELD EQUIPMENT AND TECHNIQUES

The types and amount of measurement equipment the researcher takes with him into the field depend largely upon the purposes of his fieldwork, the climate, the nature of the terrain, and the nature of the maps and data he can obtain from others. If the proposed study focuses upon agriculture, for example, essential equipment may include rain gauges, a soil thermometer, and soil color charts. If the climate is tropical, corrosion-resistant implements, silica gel to remove excess moisture, and special tropical packs may be the order of the day. If fording streams or climbing steep, rough terrain presents special problems, light-weight equipment is necessary. An important step in planning equipment needs, therefore, is to seek the advice of those who have done similar research in nearby areas. Such checking might, for example, have spared past researchers the grief of having their too-beautiful rain gauges turn up as the personal adornment of informants.

Whether you have in mind the project outlined at the end of this chapter or some future research in "faraway places with strange-sounding names," there is one piece of valuable and complex measuring equipment always present: your own body. We suggested earlier that the potential fieldworker should get to know himself as a tool, and this suggestion applies to measurement. Measures of distance commonly used are the breadth or length of a finger, the thumb, or a specific joint; the span from the thumb to either the tip of the little finger or the tip of the index finger; from the top of the middle finger to the elbow (usually about eighteen inches, this is the unit called a cubit); or over outstretched arms from fingertip to fingertip (the fathom); or various kinds of paces. Knowing the equivalents in inches for several of these units enables you to measure in the field even when you may be "travelling light" and have no other measuring devices available.

In sketch mapping, the main method for measuring distance is pacing. Surveyors or those who do a great deal of mapping learn to adjust their pace to equal one yard. While this method is convenient because it facilitates the conversion of figures from paces to yards and inches, it is not recommended for anthropological fieldwork because it takes considerable practice to maintain an even one-yard pace when the researcher is tired and shortens his step, or when the terrain is very uneven.

The sketch mapper usually finds it desirable to use his natural pace and convert it to the equivalent number of inches or centimeters. The length of a person's natural walking pace is extraordinarily uniform, as may be tested by counting your paces along a street block or some measured course a number of times. It will vary somewhat if you are hurrying, if you are tired, if you are wearing high heels, if you are carrying heavy or bulky objects, or if the terrain is rough. As one cartographer has noted, however, "the human legs are quite an efficient measuring mechanism." However, as soon as one begins to count his paces they become unnatural; practice is required to pace unconsciously. Greenhood suggests, "The next time you are out walking, let the notion come over you to count every time your right foot comes down. Whether you are in town or in the country, just count, or grunt, or squeak every time your right foot comes down. Keep doing this until it becomes a habit, kind of mechanical" [1964]. Counting only every second step reduces the counting but does not completely release the mind from concentration. If the distances to be paced are fairly long, you may want to use a pedometer, a small instrument that registers each forward step and shows the total distance covered on a dial.

An alternative to pacing that gives good results is measurement with the use of a wheel—a bicycle if one is available for your fieldwork. It is easy enough to find the factor of the bicycle wheel by riding it over a measured distance. Revolutions of the wheel can be counted by tying a little piece of cane or a springy twig to the front wheel so it will give a twang at each revolution as it passes the forks. The main problem with bicycle measurement is that it is much harder to cycle straight than to walk straight, so a margin for error must be allowed.

Another method is the time-honored one of "chaining," measuring a length by laying a cord, chain, or tape down successively along the survey line. This involves the assistance of a second person.

For some kinds of distance measurements, many researchers like to use pocket rangefinders, which can be inexpensive and relatively accurate. As an alternative, use the rangefinder on your camera if that does not upset people or make them feel they are continually being photographed.

There are times when a good photograph may make an important contribution to a map, provided some requirements are met: the position of the camera must be known, and the camera must be held truly level. Include something that shows scale in your photographs. Vertical aerial photos, where available, are a great boon to the map maker. In recent years, landscape sketching, once a cherished art of geographers and some archaeologists, has fallen into disuse. Photography provides such quick means of obtaining pictures that few people carry sketchpads into the field. Field sketching has advantages over photography in some respects, however, in that it stimulates close observation, it makes possible the elimination of foreground obstructions, it facilitates the selection of significant features, and labels and explanations can be placed right on the picture.

DRAWING THE MAP

If you are fortunate, you may be able to start with someone else's map. Copying, even tracing, is a common procedure in both military and civilian mapping, not because of laziness but to make use of good work that has already been done. Remember, however, there are copyright laws. Road maps, for example, usually bear a copyright but even in such cases, you may use the information the map provides if you do not use the maker's particular design, special symbols of his own invention, his interpretation and expression of detail, or copyrighted typeface designs. Identify the source of any material that is not common knowledge or does not come from good public authority. In general, identification of source materials helps to establish the quality of your map. In most cases, when a cartographer working for the

United States government makes a map, you may use it as a base map. In this country there are more than twenty federal offices publishing maps, among them the Geological Survey, Coast and Geodetic Survey, General Land Office, and the Hydrographic Survey. Some, including the Hydrographic Survey, have maps of foreign as well as domestic areas. While planning foreign fieldwork, mention a desire to obtain maps in your contacts with embassy officials. In cases where army maps are involved, for example, negotiations may be on a government-to-government level.

Whether you are starting from scratch to create your own map or using the work of others, bear in mind the nature of your project and the related purposes of your map. The selection of important features and the playing down or elimination of nonessential ones is a vital part of map construction. Some ethnographers suggest that a fairly detailed map may be useful while gathering raw data because it reminds both informant and researcher of relationships in several realms. In general, however, uncluttered maps are best at later stages. Your first completed map will be a satisfying job, a lively expression of the facts of life in the community; but be sure not to attempt too much on a single map. Remember, too, that the maps produced by anthropologists in their published reports are intended as supplements to the reports, not as independent works.

Choosing the scale of the map you will produce is closely related to all of these matters because the scale sets limits on the amount of information that can be included and how it can be shown. All maps are reductions, but too small a size may overly limit the things you can represent. Too large a scale makes for problems, as anyone who has wrestled with maxi-maps in mini-autos knows. Again, you should be guided by the purpose of the map, making sure that the essential features can be handled adequately. Of course, in the field, portability is important. (It will also be important for your instructor when you complete Project 2!) An obvious alternative, when one has a wealth of detail to include but wants to avoid cluttering, might be to make two maps of the area, each showing a different category of information.

A cartographic draftsman who does freehand lettering, can use special pens, lettering sets, and all of the other necessary tools of the trade, and is knowledgeable about transfer patterns, papers, and so on, is rare—and, characteristically, very popular around anthropology departments. A lack of such manual skills and training, however, should not keep anyone from learning the principles of graphic expression. At some point, you may want to consult with or use the talents of a skilled draftsman in postfield phases of your work. You may also want to call on a cartographer, especially if you plan to publish maps. A cartographer evaluates and rectifies data, and can make suggestions regarding the presentation of data on the basis of modern theories concerning reactions to visual stimuli, and so on.

Since we consider only simple sketch mapping of the type most ethnographers would expect to do in the field, there are no discussions of surveying or the types of expensive and complicated equipment it might entail. For more advanced information, particularly with regard to surveying, Spier [1970], Detweiler [1948], and the Boy Scouts of America [1960] are suggested.

THE PROJECT

Construct a basic map or chart that you could later use in conducting a field study. You may chart a whole village, or a segment of an urban or suburban area. It must be a real place with real people; and the assignment must take you into "the field." Please bear in mind that you want your map to be as useful as possible in connection with an investigation of the lifeways and interaction of the people who live there. Include such items as railroads, roads and paths, bus depots, utilities, shops, the offices of doctors and lawyers, public clinics, police stations, firehouses, postal facilities, schools, churches, government offices, cemeteries, warehouses and factories. Your completed map should give anyone who consults it a good idea of the settlement patterns of those who live there and the placement of the human and physical resources available to them. Choice of the exact kinds of items to be placed on the map is largely left to you. Perusing the maps in some ethnographies may suggest categories you would like to consider. Note that the map or chart you are constructing may include areas that are markedly different in ethnic composition, degree of economic well-being, population density, household size, or other important variables of which an anthropologist should be aware as he plans his research. Any such important features should be treated in your map. Please note that we have used the words "map" and "chart." Unless you are able to work with good aerial photographs or official maps as the basis of your project, it would be best to refer to the product you create originally as a chart, rather than a map, to indicate its lack of technical complexity. To accompany your chart or map, write a small statement to describe ways in which the area you have charted and its resources relate to places and people nearby. You might include information about changes that have taken place in the area, based on conversations and interviews with its residents.

The three maps included with this chapter were created for different purposes and in very different areas. One is from a sketch made by a student conducting an ethnographic study in an Asian community. Another, sketched by a student member of a team conducting an archaeological dig in a coastal Mexican community, illustrates the context of the dig. The third is the only one included that shows an anthropologist's use of published maps as a starting point. In this case, an urban anthropologist working in the Middle East used a published map, but constantly checked and corrected it, constructing his own maps to show changes that had been made and cultural features not on the cartographer's map. In this case, the anthropologist then asked several native residents to draw their own sketches of the community. Their maps gave the field-worker a far clearer idea of how people see their community and those features that they stress as important parts of their culture. This idea might be possible for you to pursue also, if you have the time. Talking with people about your project might also encourage them to mention features of which you are not aware, or open some doors to you.

Although the urban map included in this chapter shows a whole city, it is not expected that those of you working in urban areas should attempt to map a whole city. The extent of the area within a city that you map might best be decided in consultation with your instructor, on the basis of the density of population and/or on the basis of being able to delineate and map one culturally distinct section within the city. In the absence of specific guidelines, eight square blocks in a city might prove a good area with which to work. Please note that a section of a city might not have present within it all of the cultural features that we suggested above might be placed on your map. You might then find it important to indicate more fine-grain details. Bear in mind that you want to show those things that bear upon human interrelationships, or channel how humans move within the area in question. It might then be relevant to show such things as bus stops, street lights, directional signs, direction of traffic flow, and police- and fire-call boxes.

Please remember the following four things that should be part of your map:

- orientation
- an indication of the scale used
- date of the map
- a key or legend

△	temple
□	school
══	road
⬭	settlement
C	'commune headman' residence
1 - 7	numbered <u>mùubâan</u>
-- -- --	boundary of <u>mùubâan</u>
—.—..	boundary of 'commune'
━━━	boundary of 'district'
〜〜	river
〜〜	irrigation canal
———	20-meter contour line

Figure 2–1

Schematic map of the study village--"Old Pavilion"

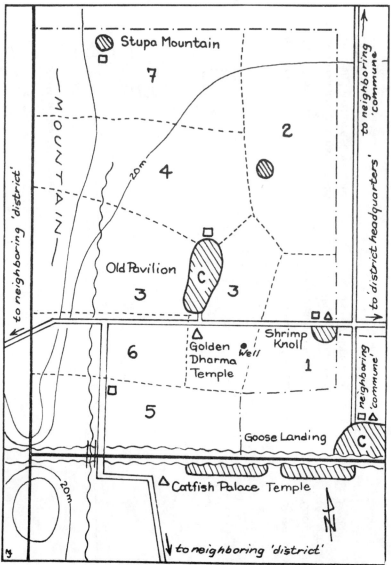

Source: From James Nelson Riley, *Family Organization and Population Dynamics in a Central Thai Village*, unpublished Ph.D. dissertation, University of North Carolina, Chapel Hill, 1972, by permission of James Nelson Riley. Redrawn by Maria Jorrin.

Figure 2-2

Sketch Map of a Mexican Coastal Village

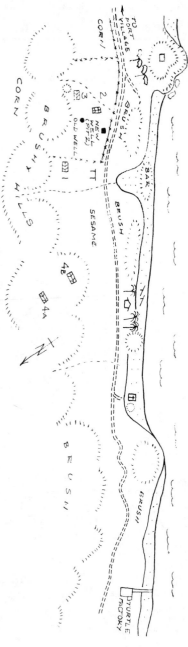

⊤⊤ Shelter for corn

⊞ Shrine of the Cross

⊞ Houses: 1, Cervantes; 2, Ernesto's son;
3, Don Ernesto; 4A, Vasquez;
4B, Vasquez' son

⇨ American's house

⅄ Beach shelters

◻ Pumphouse for
Port Village water

🍌 Banana grove

🌴 Coconut plantation
(American owned)

⋰ Cockpit

Source: By Maria Jorrin. A graduate student's map of the community in which she was a member of a group
conducting an archaeological dig.

ANTHROPOLOGY FIELD PROJECTS

Figure 2-3

Map of Tripoli, Lebanon, 1961

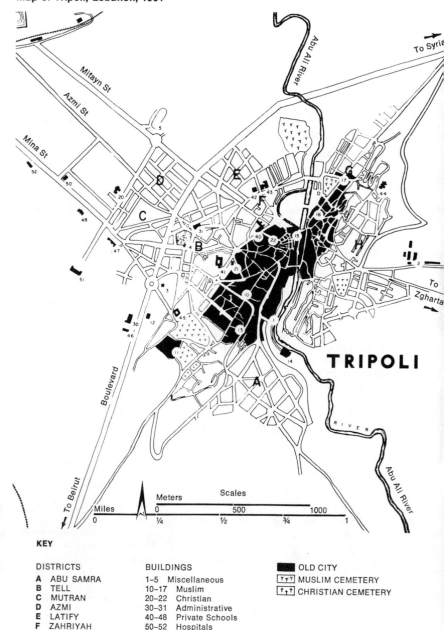

KEY

DISTRICTS
- **A** ABU SAMRA
- **B** TELL
- **C** MUTRAN
- **D** AZMI
- **E** LATIFY
- **F** ZAHRIYAH
- **G** BAB AT-TIBBANI
- **H** AL-QUBBAH

BUILDINGS
- 1–5 Miscellaneous
- 10–17 Muslim
- 20–22 Christian
- 30–31 Administrative
- 40–48 Private Schools
- 50–52 Hospitals

■ OLD CITY
⟨ᵀᵧᵀ⟩ MUSLIM CEMETERY
⟨✝₊✝⟩ CHRISTIAN CEMETERY

Source: From "Images of an Arab City" by John Gulick, pp. 179–197, *Journal of the American Institute of Planners*, August 1963, vol. 29, no. 3. Reprinted by permission of the Journal of the American Institute of Planners.

While a fancy "compass rose" design showing compass points is not necessary, there should be at least an arrow to indicate direction. Since every map is a reduction, an indication of the scale is an absolute necessity. Visual "bar scales" are favored over such statements as "one inch equals one mile," because when the map is reproduced a change in size will be reflected equally in the map and in the scale notation. It is as important to date your map as it is to date the other materials you create in the field, especially because almost all boundaries change from time to time, and it is difficult to search out the minor changes. Also, if you do future fieldwork in the same area and create a series of maps over time, you may have an indication of the rate of certain changes, as well as the direction of change. A good symbol is a conventional design that can be recognized without a legend. Such a symbol is either reminiscent of the feature it represents or has been established by long use in mapping. Even with good symbols, some kind of legend for at least a portion of the features of the map is usually necessary.

SELECTED ANNOTATED BIBLIOGRAPHY

Boy Scouts of America
> *Surveying.* New Brunswick, New Jersey: Boy Scouts of America, 1960. Straightforward, clear, and very inexpensive.

Debenham, Frank
> *Map Making.* London: Blackie, 3rd ed., 1956. A clear and thorough source, written by a British geographer.

Detweiler, A. Henry
> *Manual of Archaeological Surveying.* New Haven, Connecticut: American Schools of Oriental Research, 1948. The only manual exclusively on this topic, it is thorough but quite technical.

Finch, James K.
> *Topographic Maps and Sketch Mapping.* Wiley, 1920. A standard reference but not new.

Greenhood, David
> *Mapping.* University of Chicago Press, 1964. A readily available paperback, often used in beginning courses in cartography.

Holmes, Lowell D.
> *Anthropology: An Introduction.* Ronald, 2nd ed., 1971. A pleasantly written little text whose chapter on fieldwork in general and mapping in particular makes good reading.

Low, J. W.
> *Plane Table Mapping.* Harper, 1952. A standard work on its topic—but probably more than you will require for some time.

Maranda, Pierre
    Introduction to Anthropology: A Self-Guide. Prentice-Hall, 1972. Included here because of its mapping project.
Melbin, Murray
    "Mapping Uses and Methods." In Richard N. Adams and Jack J. Preiss, eds., *Human Organization Research.* Dorsey, 1960. Contains some good suggestions, relevant for anthropology.
Monkhouse, F. J., and H. R. Wilkinson
    Maps and Diagrams, Their Compilation and Construction. London: Methuen, 1952. A standard reference on the subject.
Raisz, Erwin
    General Cartography. McGraw-Hill, 1938. A classic by a geographer's geographer.
Robinson, Arthur H., and Randall D. Sale
    Elements of Cartography. Wiley, 3rd ed., 1969. A good, solid reference.
Spier, Robert F. G.
    Surveying and Mapping: A Manual of Simplified Techniques. Holt, Rinehart and Winston, 1970. Written for anthropologists, particularly archaeologists, by an expert—and an ingenious gadgeteer.

PROJECT THREE
CHARTING KINSHIP

INTRODUCTION

Kinship is the topic anthropologists have studied more than any other. This is because in the preliterate societies which anthropologists have traditionally studied knowledge of the kinship system is crucial for an understanding of how each society is structured and how it functions economically, politically, ritually, and so on.

Modern anthropologists now conduct their research in societies on every level of sociocultural development from the most primitive to the most highly developed. While it is true that in modern, highly developed societies kinship ties are generally less important for large-scale organization, kinship remains an important aspect of social relations. As one anthropologist says:

> The family is man's most basic, most vital, and most influential institution. It is the foundation of society, the molder of character and personality, and the mentor of cultural values . . . . Family is what makes the differences between a "house" and a "home." It is in the family that man first learns to walk, to talk, and to function as a human being. It is where he learns the values that will influence his behavior all his life as he deals with the greater society. And it is where one acquires his self-image and his goals and his ideas of what he himself will someday seek in the way of a spouse and a home [Holmes 1971, p. 358].

It is the kinship system that determines the make-up of the

family—in other words, how new members are recruited into the family (by birth, by adoption, by marriage, etc.), how the off-spring are brought up, and how inheritance of property or position is regulated.

The ways in which people are assigned by their societies to various social groups are often quite different from the practices in the Western societies with which most of us are familiar, and even from the ways suggested by objective biological facts. Consequently, this may be the first major item about which beginning anthropology students have difficulty in suspending their ethnocentric biases. For example, in many societies a person is not automatically assigned to the sex group for which we would consider him or her biologically determined. Among the Comanche and other warlike Plains tribes, those men to whom a warrior's career was repulsive were permitted to put on women's clothes and become accomplished at women's tasks. Nor is one always assigned to an age grouping that has very much to do with the time that has elapsed since one was born. The nature of kinship ties also varies from one society to another. A society may ignore or restrict natural "blood" ties or define them in ways that seem "unnatural" to us. It may artificially create a bond of kinship, or it may expand a natural bond to an indefinite extent.

The first important developments in the methodology of collecting kinship data and presenting them diagrammatically came from W. H. R. Rivers, whose "genealogical method" was first published in 1910. This method remains the foundation for most subsequent anthropological research on kinship systems. Rivers, like many researchers before and after him, found that most people enjoy talking about their relatives, past and present. Collecting genealogies, therefore, gives the fieldworker a convient entry into a society, as well as providing him with important data about the basic structures on which the society is built.

Rivers used as few terms referring to kinship ties as possible in his first step, the collection of a person's "pedigree." He limited himself to using only terms for father, mother, child, husband, and wife. He began, for example, by asking his Solomon Island informant Kurka the names of his father and mother, making it clear that he wanted the names of the people who gave rise to Kurka's being, not anyone else who might be called by the same kinship terms. After learning that Kurka's father, Kulini, had had only one wife and his mother, Kusua, only one husband, he obtained the names of their children in order of age, and so on. He "found it convenient to record the names of males in capital letters and those of females in ordinary type" [1910, p. 2]. Thus he constructed a chart some of the features of which, as you will see, are still used in making genealogical charts. Kurka's chart looked in part as follows:

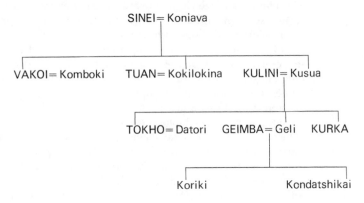

Rivers then used this chart with people's given names to collect Kurka's terms of reference for his relatives. Terms of reference are those used in speaking to someone about a third person, in the form "He is my _____." Of course, like modern anthropologists, Rivers collected such genealogies from many members of the community in order to get an overview of the whole kinship structure.

CHARTING KINSHIP TODAY

Modern anthropological kinship charts look different from those created by Rivers, although the basic principles and purposes of their construction remain the same. There are three basic kinds of relatives a person can have, all of whom may be found on his kinship chart. Consanguineal and affinal relatives can be found on every complete chart, and many include fictive kin as well. Anthropologists term the genetic connections between people "consanguineal" relationships. This means literally a "blood" relationship, although we are all aware, of course, that genes, not blood, transmit hereditary characteristics. Your consanguineal relatives, then, include your mother, your father, your grandmother, your grandfather, your son and daughter, the uncles and aunts who are the brothers and sisters of your parents, and so on. Affinal relatives are those to whom relationship is traced through a marriage link. Your affinal relatives, then, include your spouse, your in-laws, and the spouses of your parents' siblings. A large number of societies also recognize fictive kin. Fictive kin, simply stated, are those persons to whom ties are created where no consanguineal or affinal tie exists. The fiction may, however, have considerable importance and legal backing in a particular society. In our society the best example of fictive kin is an adopted child. "Ritual kin," those linked by ceremonial ties, include godchildren, blood brothers, and so on, who are characteristically thought of as one type of fictive kin.

Diagrams of kinship ties are much more convenient and easily understood than verbal descriptions. It takes very little practice to understand and use diagrams. The symbols for male and female used by anthropologists are, for example, merely more convenient forms of the Mars [♂] and Venus [♀] symbols utilized by biologists and made familiar by the women's liberation movement. There are four basic components:

$\triangle$ male

$\bigcirc$ female

$=$ affinal, or marriage, tie

| or —   consanguineal tie

Note, then, that single lines are used to tie together all of the people who are genetically related to one another.

Difference in generation level is shown by running the single line down from parents to their offspring. Siblings (brothers and sisters) are placed along a single horizontal line from left to right in order of birth. Using the four components, the following diagram shows a family consisting of a father, mother, son, and daughter.

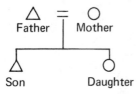

The family we have diagrammed is known as a "nuclear family." The nuclear family, consisting of a pair of parents and their offspring, is a basic building block of kinship in almost all societies. Most people belong to two nuclear families during the course of their lives, the family in which one is raised as a child (the *nuclear family of orientation*), and the family one founds when one marries and has children of one's own (the *nuclear family of procreation*). To illustrate this for the daughter in the chart above, she might have two nuclear families as follows:

nuclear
family of
orientation

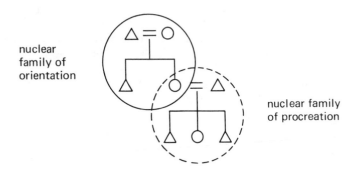

nuclear family
of procreation

The daughter's chart would be very confusing if we had not already suggested from whose viewpoint the chart was being constructed, and if we had not further clarified matters by circling and labelling the families. The people of the oldest generation might, for example, be thought of as grandfather and grandmother, as father and mother, or as father-in-law and mother-in-law by other people shown on the chart. To avoid such confusion every chart must be considered from the viewpoint of one, and only one, person. In every chart, then, one must show who is the point of entry into the chart, the person who is the central subject from whose viewpoint the chart is constructed. (See example below.) This person, called "Ego," is so labelled, or the

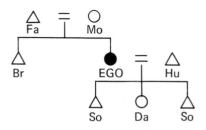

ANTHROPOLOGY FIELD PROJECTS

symbol for the person is shaded, or both. Once we know who is Ego, we can correctly label the other symbols in the diagram. To save space and effort, it is conventional to use abbreviations that are simply the first two letters of the shortened word.

You may need other symbols for your charts, such as the following:

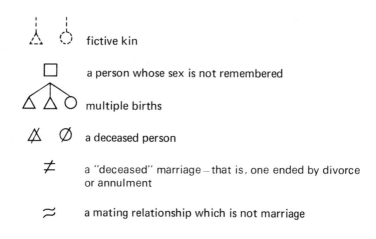

A chart for an imaginary individual is given on the following page to illustrate ways of using all of the symbols.

THE PROJECT

Interview someone and make as complete a genealogical chart for him or her as possible. If possible, work with an informant from another culture who can talk about his kinship in another language as well as in English, and who has a reasonably large number of relatives. Assign appropriate terms to each individual—the full name, the term of reference, such as "cousin" (the term your informant would use in referring to the relative while speaking with a third party), and the term he uses for address, such as "Mom," "Slim," "Uncle Joe." (Terms of address are, as you see, the terms one uses when speaking to the person in question.) For the sake of clarity, it is suggested that you place the terms of address in quotation marks. If the informant did not know the person and therefore had no

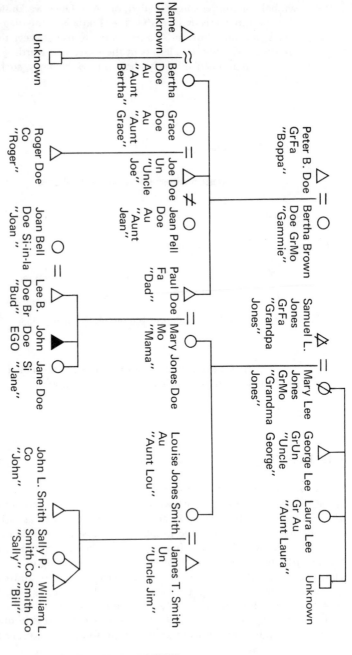

term of address for him or her, you may simply draw a line to indicate the lack of a term.

One kind of analysis that you can make even on the basis of a rather simple kinship chart is to test the common assumption that terms equating individuals reflect behavioral equivalences, and that terms differentiating individuals reflect behavioral differences. In American English usage, for example, terms such as "uncle," "aunt," or "cousin" group together the relatives on both the mother's and father's sides of the family. Use of the term "cousin" goes one step farther and groups together male and female relatives. Ask your informant in what instances "lumping" people under a single term reflects social and behavioral equivalences toward such relatives—or whether they are socially and behaviorally distinguished. Discuss how his relatives have been recruited—by marriage, adoption, and so on, and the groups from which they came. Does he have fictive kin? If so, what is the nature of their ties to one another? Of course, if your informant's chart reveals patterns that are different from those you know well, you should follow the information and ask the questions that suggest themselves to you as most likely to lead to a clear exposition of what lies behind the terms collected.

SELECTED ANNOTATED BIBLIOGRAPHY

Please note that most of the references given below are mainly for the convenience of those who want to read somewhat more widely on the subject. Only the Schusky reference is suggested as particularly valuable for "chartsmanship" and the work of the project.

Bohannan, Paul, and John Middleton, eds.
    Kinship and Social Organization. Natural History Press, 1968. A well-chosen and readable selection.
Graburn, Nelson, ed.
    Readings in Kinship and Social Structure. Harper & Row, 1971. One of the many collections of basic articles on these topics. This one is mentioned particularly for the student who may wish to do more extensive reading on his own because it contains good introductions to sections that tie together the history of thought in this area.
Holmes, Lowell D., ed.
    Readings in Anthropology. Ronald, 1971. One of the many good basic readers, this one is mentioned because of the material on the family it includes.
Murdock, George P.
    Social Structure. Macmillan, 1949. A classic in the field, this book incorporates a statistical approach in comparing systems from worldwide samples.

Rivers, W. H. R.

"The Genealogical Method of Anthropological Inquiry." *The Sociological Review*, 3:1–12. The article that started it all—referred to at length in the discussion of this project.

Schusky, Ernest L.

Manual for Kinship Analysis. Holt, Rinehart and Winston, 2nd ed., 1972. Compact, concise, clear, readily available, and inexpensive, this is the single reference most used by anthropology students.

PROJECT FOUR

INTERVIEWING INFORMANTS

INTRODUCTION

An anthropologist in the field is concerned with getting to know as many people as possible in the community he is studying. If the group is reasonably small (as, for example, a hunting and gathering band or a peasant village), he can easily meet everyone, and get to know each member as an individual. His descriptions of the community, therefore, will be based on his repeated observations, and on the information gathered from all (or, at least, from a large number) of these individuals.

Any member of the group under study who provides information for the fieldworker is called an "informant"; but the anthropologist asks his several informants to perform different services, on the basis of his own particular research interests and on the basis of the informants' individual abilities, areas of special knowledge, and availability. In the early days of anthropological fieldwork in the United States, it was frequently impossible to meet and speak with all the members of the community because the community had ceased to exist. When it came to recording the cultures of almost-vanished North American Indian tribes, for instance, the anthropologist often had to settle for the recollections of one or two old survivors of the tribe that used to be. In many cases these survivors were the only sources of information about the cultures of departed groups the anthropologist had. Therefore, the ethnographer working with informants of this time was able to investigate only a randomly remembered past of the culture in which he was interested.

In other cases, anthropologists were unable to work with everyone, even if the communities they studied were still intact. Limitations of time, money, equipment, and other research resources sometimes made it necessary for the anthropologist to select one or two members of the group to interview in depth. He would then try to select people who seemed to have a knowledge of the ways of their people, and a sensitivity for what the anthropologist was trying to do that was broader and deeper than that of their fellows.

There are other reasons why it is not always possible to become personally acquainted in depth with everyone in a community. This might be the case when the anthropologist is working in a very large community, or when he is doing a study that involves the comparison of two or more different communities. There is, in addition, a pragmatic human factor. Obviously, even if it *is* possible to meet everyone and to cultivate numerous personal friendships, not everyone in every community knows everything about every aspect of his culture. Even in the "simplest" hunting and gathering societies, there will be specialists or experts—perhaps a curer who knows a great deal about medicinal plants, an especially good hunter who knows animals and hunting techniques thoroughly, an old grandparent who knows the ancient tales or songs, and so forth. In these cases, the anthropologist could make the most efficient use of his time and energy by focusing his questioning on those experts who will be able to give him the most detailed information on their various specialties.

These chosen specialists will be the fieldworker's main links to the culture under study. Although the anthropologist must, of course, talk to and observe as many people as possible, in order to get the full cultural context and the "flavor" of ordinary life in the community being studied, he can rely on one or more expert informants to provide him with the sort of detailed, specific information on various crucial aspects of the culture that will be the core of his ethnographic report.

The use of a specialized informant generally involves some sort of training process. The anthropologist must instruct the informant as to what sort of information he wants, and how he wants it recorded. This has been especially true of linguistic fieldwork, where the informant must be taught to work with a fairly complex series of techniques and symbols. A short, on-the-spot course in anthropology is almost always required whenever the ethnographer works in depth with an informant. As a result, the fieldworker must be acutely aware of the potential

Anthropologist John F. Marshall with a group of Rajputs at the funeral feast for an old woman, State of Uttar Pradesh, India. Photo by courtesy of Judith Marshall.

bias in these situations. There is a danger, of course, that the ethnographer, by telling the informant what he wants to know, and how he wants that information collected, is forcing his informant to think in a way that is unfamiliar to him. The informant may end up telling the anthropologist only what the latter has indicated he wants to hear. This is especially true when informants are also interpreters in a culture whose language the anthropologist does not speak. Some degree of structuring is inevitable, to be sure, but the anthropologist must be continually on guard, and must at all times encourage the informant to be spontaneous with his information. He should also be encouraged to make suggestions of his own as to what is and is not meaningful for his people, how *they* tend to conceptualize and categorize, and so forth.

In every human group, there are certain things that people "know," and that are relatively easy to conceptualize. For example, any of several adult men in a coastal or riverine New Guinea tribe would be able to tell the anthropologist how to build a canoe—if only because he could show the anthropologist the process in a concrete, step-by-step way. However, every culture has, above and beyond its material creations, a set of values, attitudes, sentiments (see Project 7) that are attached to those objects. For example, in his classic study of the Iatmul people of New Guinea, Bateson [1936] points out that the Naven ceremony, an elaborate and complex set of rituals, is held to celebrate a young person's first adult achievement. Thus, the building of the first canoe by a young man is cause for one of these great ritual observances. Clearly, then, the building of the canoe has more than just a pragmatic value; it is a symbolic act related in various complex ways to the religious and kinship structures of the group. Thus, while it would be easy enough to find someone to describe how to build a canoe, it might be somewhat more difficult to find an informant able to express the deeper, more abstract concepts that go along with the physical production.

A number of anthropologists despair at the ambiguity of the concept of "value," or "attitude," and the notion of the "symbol" is currently at the center of a blazing debate in certain quarters. As a result, some anthropologists feel that it is futile to attempt to elicit such information from the informant. If we cannot communicate among ourselves what we mean by a "value," how could we possibly expect an informant from another culture to inform us about his group's values? In fact, an interesting study was done by Young and Young [1961] that statistically correlated the information they received from their key informants in a rural Mexican village and cross-checked with similar information gleaned from other sources (historical documents, folklore, projective tests). They discovered that, while there was a high degree of agreement on the purely factual, concrete aspects of culture, there was very little agreement when it came to the more abstract aspects of life in the village.

Nevertheless, since anthropologists are perenially interested in what people think about as well as what they do, we must continue to ask questions about peoples' values, even though we realize the possible ambiguities of that approach. Hopefully, impressions gleaned from one's informants will be supplemented by data gained from the analysis of folklore, personal documents, or any of the several other techniques suggested in other projects in this book. No single approach to the collection of data in the field is fool-proof. The anthropologist builds up his knowledge of the culture he is studying by asking the same questions in a variety of ways.

With this caution in mind, we may still be safe in saying that interviewing informants is a central part of the field experience. Anthropologists have long talked among themselves about the intensely personal relationships that they have experienced with their informants. It is not surprising that the anthropologist, often isolated from all friends and contacts while in the field, should respond so deeply to the one or two members of the community who most actively share his work, and who are most closely involved in the day-to-day problems and projects of his study. Many an anthropologist has continued the relationship with his informants long after he has left the field. Special informants are almost always rewarded by the anthropologist; this may take the form of a cash salary, if such is appropriate in the particular culture, but it very often takes the form of exchanges of gifts or of other, more intangible favors (standing as a godparent for a child, bringing that child for education in the United States or Europe, and so forth). Most anthropologists take the position that since the informant is giving up his time and energy, he or she should be repaid in some way considered mutually appropriate and satisfactory.

In recent years, the entire topic of relations with informants has come out of the domain of private chitchat to become a distinct part of many contemporary ethnographies; Beattie's ethnography of Bunyoro [1960, 1965] and Chagnon's colorful portrait of the Yanomamo [1968] are two good examples of ethnographies in which the anthropologist's informants stand out as individual characters in their own right, and in which significant parts of the books are devoted to discussions of relations with informants. Another interesting account of this kind is Powdermaker's warm and readable *Stranger and Friend* [1960], in which she discusses her fieldwork career and the several informants she has known and worked with. *In the Company of Man* [Casagrande 1960] is a collection in which twenty anthropologists pay tribute to their respective informants by recording their life histories.

Although working with an informant is so often critical to the field research, it is not possible to walk into a village and immediately zero in on an informant. Selecting a good informant is, in its own way, a delicate art, and most profitably grows out of the participant-observation experience (see Project 5). As Pelto has noted:

> . . . through participant-observation, the fieldworker notes which persons are most involved in their actions—they are the ones with the greatest amount of firsthand information. Furthermore, he learns about informants' "stakes" in social action, so he can assess the likelihood that any given informant might distort information to maintain self-respect or for other reasons [1970, pp. 97–98].

Even after exercising the greatest care in his selection, the anthropologist may still end up with a poor informant. Certain people in the group may push themselves forward because to work with the "stranger" might enhance their prestige in their own group. Moreover, people who like to talk with the "stranger" are, as we mentioned earlier, frequently people who are shunned by their own group for one reason or another. [See Williams 1967, pp. 28–31, for a fuller discussion of these problems.]

Nevertheless, once one or more informants have been selected, and once the ethnographer is satisfied that their information is trustworthy, the process of "depth" interviewing can begin. The interview, as such, is a data-collection technique most commonly associated with psychology or sociology. In anthropology, an interview is never an isolated event, but is always a part of the participant observation process, an encounter with an individual whom one has observed in a variety of other contexts as well [Becker & Geer 1957]. Nevertheless, there is much to be learned from interviewing tactics developed in the other disciplines because they have historically been important to anthropologists in the field as well.

Generally speaking, there are two types of interview: the formal and the informal. In doing fieldwork, the anthropologist often finds that some of his best interviews are the result of chance encounters. For example, one of the authors had the experience of walking down the road to the village post office, not intending to meet anyone or discuss anything in particular. But, on the way, he saw an old man gathering stones from his yard and arranging them in patterns in his doorway. Stopping to say hello, the anthropologist soon asked what the old man was doing. He learned that the stones were meant to keep demons out of the house. This was important because his daughter-in-law had just gone into labor, and newborn babies are especially susceptible to any wandering demons who might be sent out by magicians in the employ of the family's enemies. Thus, in this chance meeting, the anthropologist learned something about certain myths and rituals, about family relationships, and about the network of factions in the village. To be sure, all of this had to be corroborated by asking others if the same beliefs, activities, and feelings held true for them as well, or if this was all the old man's individual quirk. As it turned out, the old man's belief was typical of elderly people, but was not commonly seen any more. Since the ethnographer did not deliberately seek out the old man, and since he had no idea of what, beyond the most general, questions to ask (he knew nothing about the activity prior to having witnessed it), this was an "informal" interview. Most anthropologists freely admit that a surprisingly large part of their information – sometimes the *best* information – comes from such happy accidents.

On the other hand, some interviews will be more formal in nature, since informants are frequently sought out for their particular knowledge of special topics. In many cases, the subjects will be broached in a planned fashion, often at a precisely set time of day. Even so, there are two types of formal interview that the ethnographer may choose to have with his key informant. The interview may be either structured or unstructured. The structured interview makes use of a prepared "interview schedule," a series of questions to which the anthropologist requires specific answers. Obviously, the anthropologist must himself have some experience in the culture he is studying before he can know which questions are appropriate and meaningful. In that case, the interview schedule can most effectively be used as a summation device, used to pull loose ends together toward the end of the fieldwork period. A related type of structured interview involves the use of standardized questionnaires such as that discussed in Project 11. The Health Opinion Survey in Project 11 enables the anthropologist to use a set of questions that have been validated in other research settings (or in the culture he is studying, but at an earlier date) and its main intent is to collect comparative data, to see how these people compare to people elsewhere in the world, or to see how they themselves have changed over a given period of time.

Unstructured interviews, on the other hand, allow the ethnographer to use the "happy accidents" of fieldwork to best advantage. For example, if there is a key informant chosen for his voluminous knowledge of the sugar cane industry, the anthropologist might set up an appointment to meet him in a canefield at dawn. Starting with the most general sort of question, such as

"How is cane cultivated in this district?" he can be led, step-by-step, by the specialist through the day's activities. The techniques of planting, cultivation, harvesting, and milling are both explained and, if possible, demonstrated on the spot. The interview is formal to the extent that there is an announced topic and a prepared meeting (for which, presumably, the fieldworker will be ready with notebook, tape recorder, camera, or other equipment). Some might claim that the interview is structured insofar as the anthropologist may have to guide the discussion back to the topic if the informant digresses. But if the digression is very lengthy, or if it involves a subject of grave importance to the informant, the structured interview on the prearranged topic may have to be delayed momentarily or even postponed. The anthropologist's preoccupation with the given subject should not become an obsession. If the informant is really concerned with a personal problem, or his attention has been captured by a new enthusiasm, he should be allowed to ramble in his discourse. It might cost some time and patience and upset the anthropologist's timetable, but most anthropologists feel that rigid timetables are difficult to adhere to, and that interesting information can often be gleaned from undirected discourse. Most important, the anthropologist realizes that in refusing to push the informant around in order to lead him back to the topic, he is building up good will, and acting as a good friend who is willing to take the informant's feelings and interests into account. If an informant has been well selected for his knowledge of, and interest in, a certain topic, it is virtually assured that he will want to talk about it, in detail and at length, sooner rather than later, particularly since he will likely be pleased that the foreign guest feels that he can learn something of value from him.

In an unstructured interview, it is generally best to begin with the very broadest, most open-ended sort of question, and then fill in with specifics as one's own knowledge of the topic grows. Thus, one might start with such an extremely broad question as, "Tell me about sugar cultivation around here." This general query may yield a general response such as, "Well, we plant the cane when the wet season begins in June, harvest it at the beginning of the dry season in January, and then take it to the mill over the hill, where it is processed and later sold, mainly as brown sugar or molasses." Vague and sketchy as this is, it is full of information, and provides clues for more specific questions, questions that are more likely to be intelligent now that there is some background to them. For example, "You say 'we' plant in June; who are the 'we' who plant? Do you plant seeds or shoots? Tell me how you do it." The informant replies, "In this district, the land is owned by the government sugar company and they hire only adults, both men and women. But the men and women work separately in the fields. Usually the new crop is cultivated from the part of the cane left in the ground from last year's harvest. We call this 'ratooning' the crop. The tips of the plants are stuck in the earth in rows, a few inches apart, and the area is cleared of all weeds, using a steel machete, every once in a while until the crop is ready to be harvested." This response may lead to even more specific questions: "Do the men and women do different work?" "What do they do about the snakes and scorpions that hide in the weeds?" "Suppose the part left in the ground is no longer good—now do they begin anew?" In this way, all the details of the process eventually are brought to light.

Some anthropologists have found it helpful to use the camera to record someone doing something (planting a crop, making a wagon wheel, performing a ritual) in moment-to-moment detail. Then, once the excitement and bustle of the event itself is over, he and the informant can sit down at leisure and discuss and review everything that went on, using the photos as memory aids. Another useful means of approaching the interview is for the anthropologist to ask the informant, "Could you show me how to make a fishnet (make a stone axe, cook a curry, build a barn, etc., etc.)?" In this way, he is not merely an inquisitive pest, but a friend who is willing to try to help in doing something productive.

The first aim of interviewing an informant about some aspect of production, whichever means of approach are chosen, is to get at the mechanics of the process. Unless the anthropologist already knows a great deal about the culture, it is unwise, for example, for him to go up to an arrow-maker and say, "Tell me about the magic you make to keep your arrows strong." It is usually less threatening to the informant to start with the public aspect of his craft—what materials he uses, how he fashions them into the product, and so forth—than with something that may be a very private aspect of his craft. (Of course, there are no general rules about such things. It is conceivable that, in some cultures, the magico-spiritual elements may be so clear-cut and so explicit that the informant himself might choose to start the discussion with them.)

In any case, one of the main jobs of the anthropologist as he settles into his community and begins to understand its ways of life is to find out:

- what people do in the culture under study
- how they do it
- what they think about the place of their product or service in the larger scheme of things

The depth interview with the specialist is one means of getting at these three aspects of culture. One curious result of this is that, at the end of his field study, the anthropologist often has more specialized knowledge about more areas of the culture than any one person in that culture, each of whom may be a specialist in only one area. In addition, learning how and why peoples do certain things and experiencing the frustrations of trying to do them are fine cures for ethnocentrism.

THE PROJECT

Your project is to select a specialist who will agree to be your informant in showing you how to do a particular thing, and in discussing with you the social and cultural implications of that thing. Do not choose a skill or craft that requires a great deal of abstract explication; for example, do not select a concert pianist and ask him in one interview to explain how he plays a Chopin étude. Rather, choose someone with a craft that results in a concrete product. Interviewing an informant can, of course, be used to learn about a great variety of topics, abstract as well as concrete. But it is best to begin to hone your data-gathering skills with a topic that is relatively accessible. Find out, for example, how to make a macrame belt, fashion a piece of jewelry, make a dress, construct a cabinet, prepare a gourmet dinner, plant a vegetable garden, style a hair-do, build a model airplane, etc. Be sure that your informant is one who does this thing frequently, as a profession or an ongoing hobby, and who knows something about it beyond following directions in a how-to manual.

Your report should be in two parts. The first should be a step-by-step description of how the product is fashioned, including a description of all materials and tools used. You may use a sequence of photos (see Project 13) accompanied by explanatory captions. Whether or not you use photographs or drawings, be sure that your details are *specific and clear*, as if you were describing the customs of an exotic group to an audience that was almost completely unfamiliar with either the materials used or the finished product. Therefore, it might be a good idea to choose someone who creates a product with which you are personally unfamiliar, so you will be less apt to take details for granted. The object of this exercise is to sharpen your powers of observation and description, and also to train you to ask more and more precise questions of your subject.

The second part should be a somewhat more general discussion of what the informant does with his product, what he thinks the worth of it might be, how he interacts with the people who buy or use his product, and how he came to make these products in the first place. The precise nature of the questions you ask will, of course, depend on the type of person you are interviewing, and on the type of work he does. In general, however, you should attempt to find out the values and attitudes that are attached to this craft in the informant's society.

SELECTED ANNOTATED BIBLIOGRAPHY

Bateson, Gregory
    Naven. Cambridge, England: The University Press, 1936. A classic work in social anthropology, used in this chapter to illustrate the varieties of informant knowledge with regard to a particular culture.
Beattie, John
    Bunyoro: An African Kingdom. Holt, Rinehart and Winston, 1960. A good example of an ethnography in which the anthropologist makes explicit his informant relationships.
Beattie, John
    Understanding an African Kingdom: Bunyoro. Holt, Rinehart and Winston, 1965. A review of the methods used in the performance of one particular field study. Includes some interesting comments on the cultivation of informants.
Becker, Howard S., and Blanche Geer
    "Participant Observation and Interviewing: A Comparison." *Human Organization,* 1957, 16(3):28–32. A comparison between the standard sociological and anthropological techniques of eliciting data from informants.
Bunzel, Ruth
    The Pueblo Potter: A Study of Creative Imagination. Columbia University Press, 1929. A classic study of a craftsman's sociocultural environment.
Casagrande, Joseph B., ed.
    In the Company of Man: Twenty Portraits of Anthropological Informants. Harper, 1960. Twenty anthropologists' life histories of their main informants.

Chagnon, Napoleon A.
> *Yanomamo: The Fierce People*. Holt, Rinehart and Winston, 1968. A lively and readable ethnography with insights into how the anthropologist elicits information from informants under what may seem extremely adverse field conditions.

Dean, John P., and William F. Whyte
> "How Do You Know if the Informant Is Telling the Truth?" *Human Organization*, 1958, 17(2):34–38. A concise but insightful summary of behavior and attitudes that the fieldworker might well be aware of when interviewing.

Hyman, Herbert H., et al.
> *Interviewing in Social Research*. University of Chicago Press, 1954. Geared mainly for formal interviewing (public opinion surveys), but note especially Appendix A, which discusses the selection of interviewers, and includes case histories of particular interview situations. Note also Chapter VII on "Reduction and Control of Error."

Merton, Robert K., Marjorie Fiske, and Patricia L. Kendall
> *The Focused Interview: A Manual of Problems and Procedures*. The Free Press, 1956. Geared more toward sociology than anthropology, but with some helpful comments and suggestions.

Paul, Benjamin D.
> "Interview Techniques and Field Relationships." In A. L. Kroeber, ed., *Anthropology Today*. University of Chicago Press, 1953. Although written from the general point of view of the ethnographer working in an exotic culture, this is still a valuable, concise summary of the participant-observation experience, and one that is quite applicable to fieldwork in some segments of our own society.

Pelto, Pertti J.
> *Anthropological Research: The Structure of Inquiry*. Harper & Row, 1970. A standard compendium of field methods and their theoretical foundations, noted here for the discussion on interviewing, pages 95–98.

Powdermaker, Hortense
> *Stranger and Friend*. W. W. Norton, 1966. A warm and readable discussion of this anthropologist's career and of the several informants she has known and worked with.

Royal Anthropological Institute of Great Britain and Ireland
> *Notes and Queries on Anthropology*. London: Routledge and Kegan Paul, 6th ed., 1967. A handy reference work which is often helpful to the fieldworker. It is a categorization of questions to ask on the most commonly researched topics among anthropologists, and is thus a good check-list for interviews.

Williams, Thomas Rhys
> *Field Methods in the Study of Culture*. Holt, Rinehart and Winston, 1967. A concise guide to field methods, focusing on the author's personal experiences among the Dusun of Borneo. See especially Chapter III.

Young, Frank W., and Ruth C. Young
> "Key Informant Reliability in Rural Mexican Villages." *Human Organization*, 1961, 20(3):141–148. An interesting study that statistically correlates information received from key informants in a Mexican village with information gleaned from other sources.

PROJECT FIVE

PARTICIPANT OBSERVATION

INTRODUCTION

If any technique for field research can be said to be the most characteristic anthropological contribution to social and behavioral science, it is that of participant observation. Participant observation is field research in which the ethnographer is not merely a detached observer of the lives and activities of the people under study, but is also a participant in that round of activities. By becoming an active member of the community, the anthropologist need no longer be a somewhat formidable "scientific" stranger, but can become a trusted friend. By doing, insofar as is feasible, whatever it is that the people he studies are doing, he can have a first-hand experience of what such activity means to the people themselves. He loses his natural ethnocentric bias by gradually immersing himself in the day-to-day facts of life of the people with whom he is working.

Although participant observation has come to occupy a central place in almost all anthropological fieldwork, it is perhaps unfair to label this as a "technique" for field research, since such a term implies that there is one thing (or one set of related things) that one does in order to "do" participant observation. In the last analysis, one does not "do" participant observation at all, at least not in the sense that one "does" a life history, or "does" a kinship chart, photographic series, or opinion survey. Even a highly trained and experienced field anthropologist might, despite the risk of sounding unscientifically imprecise, admit that participant observation is more a state of mind, a framework for living in the field, than it is a specific program of action.

The ideal of anthropological fieldwork is the extended field study, in which the researcher spends several months (or more) of uninterrupted residence in the community under study. Pioneering anthropologists in this century, like Margaret Mead, have been credited with "taking anthropology off the mission-house veranda"; that is, they went beyond the second-hand information gleaned from missionaries, traders, or colonial administrators and went out to live with the "natives" themselves. However, this accomplishment represented the formalization of a tendency that had been part and parcel of ethnographic practice from the beginning.

In 1800, even before there was an "anthropology" in the modern sense, the French social philosopher Joseph-Marie Degérando published a brief, and now almost completely forgotten, program for the study of other cultures. Degérando said:

> The main object, therefore, that should today occupy the attention and zeal of a truly philosophical traveller would be the careful gathering of all means that might assist him to penetrate the thought of the peoples among whom he would be situated, and to account for the order of their actions and relationships. . . . The first means to the proper knowledge of the Savages, is to become after a fashion like one of them . . . [1969, p. 70].

In one sense, the story of the adoption of the call for participant observation as the basic ethnographic strategy is a saga of the American frontier. In 1822, Henry Schoolcraft, a scholarly easterner, arrived in the frontier region of the upper Great Lakes to take up the position of Indian agent among the Chippewa (Ojibwa). His first contact was with an Irish trader named Johnson who had married an educated Chippewa woman. Schoolcraft soon became disenchanted with his "official interpreter," a besotted frontiersman with little understanding of, and absolutely no affection for, the Indians. Schoolcraft, who later married into the bicultural Johnson family, was able to get an inside view of Chippewa life. He began to understand that the errors and distortions about Indian cultures (from the "bloodthirsty savage" stereotypes of the frontiersmen to the "noble savage" romanticism of the European philosophers) were the result of constant trading in second-hand information. By living with the Indians, not merely looking at them from the outside, Schoolcraft learned that the Indian was "a man capable of feeling and affection, with a heart open to the wants and responsive to the ties of social life" [Hays 1958, p. 5].

At one point, after spending some time living in the lodges of his Indian friends, Schoolcraft discovered that the Indians created myths, tales, and legends that they told for both amusement and instruction. Although today we take it for granted that even the most technologically primitive people can possess an artistic tradition (be it graphic or verbal) of great richness and complexity, this was a revelation of the first order in Schoolcraft's day. And, more important, it was a revelation that could never have come to him in his agency office – discovering the "secrets" of the Indians required him to live among them as a friend who took part in their daily lives, participating in ordinary food-gathering forays as well as in elaborate rituals, observing them from the vantage point of one who played as active a part as possible in their "real" lives.

In the Introduction to this book we discussed the problem of ethnocentrism, which keeps people from being able to understand clearly cultures other than their own. Even some of the greatest social thinkers of the nineteenth century were explicitly ethnocentric: Freud, for example, felt that Western civilization, for all its imperfections, was the pinnacle of human achievement. Other philosophers were willing to lump the "mind of primitive man" with the thought processes of Western children and/or mental defectives.

Partly in response to these assumptions, anthropology in the twentieth century developed as an independent branch of learning. Confronted by the seemingly infinite diversity of cultures around the world, and faced with the increasingly untenable nature of the proposition that Western man alone was "right," anthropologists formulated the concept known as *cultural relativism*, which implies that we must study all cultures with the understanding that they are adequate to meet the needs of the people who live by their rules. Cultural relativism makes it inappropriate to pass moral judgments about other cultures on the basis of what is deemed appropriate in one's own. If a culture were truly "inadequate" it would not enable its people to survive, and it would disappear. While it is undoubtedly true that Eskimo culture, for example, would be inadequate to prepare an individual for life in New York City, it is no less true that the culture by which a New Yorker lives in his city from day to day would be woefully inadequate in terms of equipping one for survival in the Arctic. Of course, people other than anthropologists have also appreciated the idea of cultural relativism when they got into the field. The Danish explorer Peter Freuchen, for example, lived among the Eskimos for many years. On the very first page of his *Book of the Eskimos* [1961], he states that the Eskimos possess a sort of "extraordinary hardiness" that enables them to survive in their harsh environment. Freuchen himself was able to survive in the same environment because he learned the culture of the Eskimos and used it to help himself adapt. Each culture must be understood as a vehicle for the adaptation of people to *their own particular circumstances.* The best way to reach an understanding of the "particular circumstances" of a people is to go to live with them. Direct experience of their way of life is also the most effective way of shedding one's own ethnocentric biases.

In the early 1920s, Margaret Mead carried out pioneering fieldwork. Frustrated by the then-common insistence that certain psychological factors, notably the "storm-and-stress" of adolescence, were universal because they were found in our own society, Mead was led to investigate the people of Samoa, a Pacific island which, in the 1920s, was still relatively remote from outside influences. By going to live in the "native" village and by making herself an accepted member of a group of young Samoan girls, she was able to discover that adolescence in Samoa is marked by behavior very different from that which characterizes the teenage years in the United States. The typical situation in our society finds the burgeoning sexual feelings of teenagers buried beneath social constraints; the Samoans, on the other hand, show a great deal of tolerance for certain kinds of sexual activity among adolescents. A major conclusion of Mead's research was that Samoan adolescents do not go through the period of emotional disturbance that characterizes American and Western European adolescents, and that American and Western European young people undergo psychological reactions to specific stresses built into American and Western European cultures.

The notion of cultural relativism illustrated by Mead's findings in *Coming of Age in Samoa* [1928] and the later *Growing up in New Guinea* [1930] helped make the entire range of human behavior the legitimate subject matter of anthropology, and it gave anthropological researchers a strong reason to participate in alien life styles, as well as merely to observe them.

THE PROJECT

Although reading some of the classic ethnographies will give you a good sense of what it means to be an anthropologist in the field, only by actually becoming a participant observer in some cultural setting can anyone fully appreciate the implications of this attitude. It will, of course, be impossible for you to embark upon a sustained residence in a community in order to do this project. But, in order to get some of the "feel" of participant observation, this project will require you to spend some extra time in getting acquainted with a slightly alien cultural environment. You may, therefore, begin to be a participant observer in whatever group you select while you are doing other course work, since the formal aspects of analysis and writing can be saved until the very end.

For the purposes of this project, you are to select some activity with which you are not personally familiar. The services of a religious group with whose form of worship you are not familiar are particularly good for such an investigation, because religion is such an important social and cultural feature of the lives of so many people, and because each religion tends to have its own particular practices, customs, personnel, and so on, making it a miniature cultural system in some ways. Moreover, most individuals are likely to have a number of unconscious ethnocentric judgments regarding religious belief, so that it would be a real challenge for them to participate in the ceremonies of another religious group.

It is important to remember that you are not entering into the group's round of services merely to observe the rituals and chart the interactions — you are to be a participant in those activities as well, at least insofar as you are able to do so, given limitations on your time. This, therefore, cannot be a one-sitting project; it requires several visits, both to familiarize yourself with the rituals and personnel, and to make yourself known to members of the congregation. Therefore, you may begin making visits to the religious meetings while you are carrying out one of the other projects. It would also be helpful (and more efficient) for you to cultivate the friendship of one or more "key informants" who are especially knowledgeable about the sect, and who are likely to extend your participation by inviting you to visit the homes of members of the congregation on a social basis. In this way, you will get a more nearly rounded view of these people's lives than you would as an "objective" reporter sitting in the back of the meeting hall with your nose buried in a notebook.

The first problem involved in this project will be facing what has been defined earlier in this book as "culture shock." Even the best-trained anthropologist with experience of cultural diversity and familiar with the published sources on the people he is going off to study is apt to experience several kinds of shock (emotional as well as physical) in his first few days or weeks in the field because he is, in a very real sense, an alien, living in a social system whose cues he has not yet mastered. Of course, you will not be hit particularly hard by culture shock doing this project since you will be involved in only one aspect of an "alien" culture, and since you will be living at home or on campus while you do it. But, even so, do not be discouraged if you have a feeling of hopeless unfamiliarity at the beginning, a feeling that convinces you that there is something "wrong" going on in the service. Even so apparently trivial a situation as that of an individual raised in a sect in which one kneels to pray attending the services of a sect in which one stands or sits to pray can cause a certain degree of culture shock. The important thing is not to deny such ethnocentric feelings, but to accept them as natural, and even to verbalize them, if you wish, to a sympathetic member of the congregation. Then you can go on to learn more about the sect, so that you can understand what is going on. Eventually, rituals that initially struck you as bizarre, ridiculous, or merely different will become meaningful to you.

It is, of course, not expected that you will come to embrace fully either the rituals or the doctrines of the group you are studying. Some anthropologists have had the experience of "going native" to such an extent that they experienced reverse culture shock when they finally got home. But, no matter how much of a participant you become, you should never allow yourself to compromise your scientific objectivity. In line with this caution, it is necessary to point out that although many congregations are pleased and flattered to have an outsider express interest in their devotions, and will even welcome someone strolling in, unannounced, off the street, others with a more aggressively proselytizing outlook might logically expect that anyone who is so interested in their services might easily be converted.

If the student, then, is interested in studying a sect known for its zeal in attracting converts, it is only fair for him to speak to the minister or prominent members of the congregation beforehand to establish the fact that he is studying the group for a college course, not necessarily for his own salvation. The clergymen or members should then have the right to decide whether or not he will continue to be welcome. Although sects that are not necessarily geared to conversion or revival probably require no such formal statement of purpose at the outset, you may feel more comfortable (that is, less sneaky) if you announce your intentions at the beginning, if only to one or two key members of the congregation. If, however, you want to work with groups that depend, to one degree or another, on "secret" ceremonies (for example, the Rosicrucian orders), or that indulge in activities that may go beyond what is strictly approved by the law (for example, satanist cults), you would certainly be well advised to explain your purposes thoroughly to the leaders and then seek permission from the group before embarking on your study. In certain exotic societies, the role of "student" would be meaningless, and the anthropologist would have to find some alternate means of explaining his purpose. But, in most cases in our society, the role of student is sufficiently clear and, for the most part, readily accepted.

In all cases, your entry into the congregation would be considerably eased if you made the prior acquaintance of a member of the sect, for he could then be your initial guide, introducing you to his fellow members and reassuring them about your motives. Needless to say, your informant should be an individual who is respected and trusted by the others, if it is possible to perceive who such members are. Remember that, regardless of your own feelings about religion in general, or about this sect in particular, religion is taken very seriously by many people. Your behavior should never be cause for the disruption of any service, or for arousing any controversy among the members of the congregation.

Two sociologists, von Hoffman and Cassidy [1956–57], have described their experience in studying a Negro Pentecostal church congregation in a large city. They decided to approach the church first by playing what they thought was the anthropological game of participant observation, and they passed themselves off as potential converts. But they began to feel that this was hampering them, because they were far too concerned with role playing and defining their own place within the congregation. As they found out later on, the members of the group were by no means as concerned with them as they were with the members; and everyone was relieved when the two dropped their poses and admitted to being researchers who were happy to be part of the activity but were not integral parts of the congregation. They ruefully recalled that "participant observation has been described as the business of being a professional fifth wheel" [p. 195].

Although the several research tools described elsewhere in this book help the anthropologist to build up the information he needs to make both his description and his analysis, it is because of his participant observation activities that he is able to do ultimate justice to both the description and the analysis. The data elicited by formal surveys of whatever type are flat unless they are underscored by the perceptions of a trained and *sensitive* observer. And no analysis, no matter how statistically elegant, can be meaningful in human terms unless it has been filtered through the deeper layers of meaning that only one who has been part of the events under analysis can have. Obviously, no one can ever know a culture as well as someone who was born into it and who lives with it on a day-to-day basis. Yet most "natives" are unable to discuss and interpret their own behavior because they take so much of it for granted. Insofar as anthropology can make a special contribution to the study of human behavior, it does so because the fieldworker applies the perceptive faculties of a trained, objective observer with the personal insight of someone who has lived as a member of the group over a long period. Neither of these aspects of his professional stance should be allowed to dominate the other.

In doing this project, you will doubtless be an observer long before you feel yourself to be a real participant in the activities of the sect you have chosen. Therefore, at the outset, concentrate on being an observer. Some of the aspects which you might want to observe as closely as possible and try to describe as clearly as possible include:

- The physical layout of the service (Where is it held? How is the room arranged? What furniture or other paraphernalia are present?)
- The human dimension (How many people are attending? Relative numbers of men, women, adults, children, blacks, whites, etc.)
- Aspects of ceremonialism (time of day, specialized personnel, special objects)
- The ceremony (Who does what, when, with what, with or to whom?)

You may, if you wish, consult some encyclopedias of religion or other sources on the group you are studying, in order to help you orient yourself to the nature of the service and some of the belief system which lies behind it. But try, at this stage, to keep your observations as "pure" as possible; try to develop your own powers of careful observation, and learn to rely on them. They are the only tools that an ethnographer is always sure to have handy in the field.

After you are accepted by the congregation, and as you meet individuals whom you trust particularly as key informants, you can begin to learn from the latter:

- how they became members
- why they became members

- how often they participate
- whether they participate with family, friends, or alone

You might also get these key informants to tell you what the ceremonies are all about. You need not be concerned yet with whether their descriptions agree with yours, or whether the descriptions of ordinary members of the congregation agree with those of the minister. At this point, merely record the information as given, taking note of discrepancies.

Finally, as a result of your participation in the services, you will get to know the activities fairly well, and will be well established with many members of the congregation. Now you can begin to check the discrepancies of description. Were there things you perceived incorrectly at first because of your lack of experience? Or was the misconception on the part of the members of the congregation who, because of their deep involvement, were unable to see clearly some aspect which you, coming from the outside, perceived?

Your report should be a summary of your answers to these various questions. You may also suggest some hypotheses for further testing that might help explain some of the aspects of the services you have described and which might strike the outsider as unusual or inexplicable in some way.

One additional factor to be aware of when reporting your data is that of the potential bias arising out of the participation itself. The very presence of an outsider—no matter how friendly and how much a part of the group he may be—means that certain actions and reactions among the members of the congregation may be changed or modified. In drawing up your descriptions, try to sort out any aspects of behavior that might be the result of this type of biased behavior. Such modifications, of course, will be more frequent at the beginning of the study, when you are still something of a novelty.

Students who have access to large communities might wish to use this project to experiment a bit with the nature of participant observation data. To do this, first select a sect that has several local congregations; a good example might be several parishes of Roman Catholic churches in different neighborhoods in a city, or several congregations of Pentecostal sects scattered in a rural district. Each student in the group will take one of these congregations or parishes to study in the manner suggested above. At the end, the group will meet to compare the data collected from all the studies, in order to determine if there are any significant differences.

If there is a disparity in the descriptions presented by the several reporters, you might find it very useful to attempt to learn the reasons for such differences in conclusions. They may be attributable to one or more of the following:

- differences between the local congregations
- differences in outlook among the various observers
- differences between the observers in *method* of observation (that is, total time devoted to observation, whether one's chief informants are mostly men or mostly women, and so on)

If there does seem to be significant difference between observers, try to set down the precise areas of disagreement. Those students whose conclusions differ might then visit the congregations where others received contrasting impressions and wrote different conclusions. There is, of course, no need to force agreement among all of the members of the group on all aspects of the study. It is, however, often helpful to compare research results because you can then better understand yourself as a fieldworker. It might be useful to have a panel discussion of your several reports.

SELECTED ANNOTATED BIBLIOGRAPHY

Bowen, Elenore Smith
    Return to Laughter. Harper, 1954. A novel by a noted anthropologist, writing under a pen name, which describes the personal, ethical, and emotional adjustments of one participant observer in the field.
Bruyn, S.
    "The Methodology of Participant Observation." *Human Organization*, 1963, 22(3):224–235. A concise and detailed breakdown of the participant observation strategy.
Degérando, Joseph-Marie
    The Observation of Savage Peoples. Translated by F. C. T. Moore. University of California Press, 1969. The recently resurrected program for a participant observation approach to social anthropology. Despite the quaintness of language, Degérando's insights are startlingly contemporary and still very relevant.
Freuchen, Peter
    Book of the Eskimos. Fawcett, 1961. An explorer and adventurer discovers participant observation and becomes an amateur anthropologist.
Hays, H. R.
    From Ape to Angel. Capricorn Books, 1958. A lively and witty review of the

lives and works of some key figures in the development of anthropology; includes a fine chapter on Schoolcraft.

Hoffman, Nicholas von, and Sally W. Cassidy

"Interviewing Negro Pentecostals." *American Journal of Sociology*, 1956–57, 62:195–197. The account of two sociologists' adventures with participant observation; some excellent lessons for the field researcher working in our own society.

Jarvie, I. C.

"The Problems of Ethical Integrity in Participant Observation." *Current Anthropology*, 1969, 10:505–508.

Levi-Strauss, Claude

Tristes Tropiques. Translated by John Russell. Atheneum, 1961. One of the foremost contemporary anthropologists discusses, in a poetic and philosophical manner, what it means to do participant observation fieldwork.

Malinowski, Bronislaw

Argonauts of the Western Pacific. Dutton, 1922. One of the classic ethnographies by one of the giants of modern anthropology. In the first sections in particular, Malinowski writes with lyric eloquence and perception about how it feels to do participant observation. This is one of the most influential statements about fieldwork in the history of anthropology.

Mead, Margaret

Coming of Age in Samoa. Morrow, 1928.

Mead, Margaret

Growing Up in New Guinea. Morrow, 1930.

Paul, Benjamin D.

"Interview Techniques and Field Relationships." In A. L. Kroeber, ed., *Anthropology Today.* University of Chicago Press, 1953. Although written from the general point of view of the ethnographer working in an exotic culture, this is still a valuable, concise summary of the participant observation experience, and one that is quite applicable to fieldwork in some segments of our own society.

Vidich A., and J. Bensman

"The Validity of Field Work Data." *Human Organization*, 1954, 13(1): 20–27. The authors raise some sober and thought-provoking questions as to possible sources of bias and misinformation that can arise out of the participant observation strategy.

PROJECT SIX

COLLECTING LIFE HISTORIES

INTRODUCTION

Every complete ethnography should give the reader an understanding of the life cycle of the people in question – what it is
like to be born, to live each phase of life, and to die in that particular society. Obviously, much of the information that any anthropologist gathers in the field, because it is about a person or
people, can be useful in illuminating portions of the life cycle. It
may, of course, happen that during the anthropologist's year or
so in a particular field situation no marriages, puberty ceremonies, or funerals take place. His information about such events
must then be gathered by word of mouth only. Even if he is
afforded an opportunity to observe such things himself, he will
want to elicit people's statements about the role of such events in
their lives.

In a recent article David Mandelbaum [1973] speaks of anthropologists as having used two main approaches in their "observation of the development of a person." The first type, which
he designates "life passage (or life cycle) studies," is seen as
emphasizing the requirements of *society* and showing "how the
group socialize and enculturate their young in order to make
them into viable members of society." He points out that life-
passage events have been studied in various cultures, and cross-
cultural comparisons highlighting similarities and differences
between societies in this regard have sometimes been very valuable. (As examples, he cites Arnold van Gennep's work on rites
of passage [1909] and Margaret Mead's work on "coming of

age" in Samoa [1928] and New Guinea [1930].) Such studies have, however, tended to emphasize a single stage of life, characteristically an early one.

The second type of approach Mandelbaum mentions is that of "life history studies," which emphasize the experience and requirements of the *individual* — how the individual copes with and develops within society [Mandelbaum 1973, p. 177]. Such accounts, which follow an individual through the course of his career, are, of course, collected by people in many fields and familiar to us all as "biographies" and "autobiographies." In anthropological research, however, neither designation is really accurate, for the finished product is the result of collaboration between the subject and the anthropologist. Often the written document is set down by the anthropologist on the basis of verbal accounts by the subject. Often, too, the anthropologist must handle many problems of translation and interpretation when the subject speaks an exotic tongue or has little or no acquaintance with the written word, and he encounters problems of sequence of elicitation and presentation if the subject has no sense of chronology as we know it, and so on. For these reasons, the finished product, neither truly autobiographical nor biographical, is called a "life history" by anthropologists.

Most social scientists would strongly agree with Mandelbaum that, despite the fact that all anthropologists in the field gather a great deal of data that relate in one way or another to the "development of a person" in the society in question, there is little systematic collection and analysis of such data, and much too little attention is given to trying to combine life-passage data with life-history data from the same society in systematic and meaningful ways. Though life-passage studies have concentrated on children, life histories are almost exclusively of adults. Mandelbaum suggests that life-passage studies seldom effectively relate one stage of life to the next, personal experience to social institutions, or the exercise of personal choice to social change, although such matters are likely to be treated in a life history. With regard to life histories, he shows that, despite the urging of people in every branch of the social sciences, there have been all too few careful studies of lives as wholes, and that those that do exist lack commensurability, and, often, adequate contextual treatment and careful analysis.

Pertti Pelto points out [1970, p. 99], in the spirit of Mandelbaum's suggestions, that life histories are sometimes collected by anthropologists specifically for the purpose of relating the details and abstractions of ethnographic description to the lives of individuals. He quotes Paul Radin, who stated that his aim in collecting his well-known biography of a Winnebago Indian was "not to obtain autobiographical details about some definite personage, but to have some representative middle-aged individual of moderate ability describe his life in relation to the social group in which he had grown up." Such detailed biographies of representative individuals can then be mined for the many kinds of information they provide, including descriptive material on the life cycle. A careful blending of the two types of materials enables the ethnographer to present an especially complete and well-rounded view of life in the society in question. We do not, of course, suggest that you create for this course the kind of extensive synthesis and analysis called for by Mandelbaum and others, but want to give you some understanding of the two types of studies, their interrelationships, and their importance. The remainder of this chapter is devoted solely to life-history studies.

In the few decades just before the first life histories were collected by anthropologists—and, in fact, before anthropologists were truly anthropologists—many events took place that played an important role in determining not only what early life histories would be like, but also much of the nature and development of our discipline as a whole. Scientific knowledge of man is, on the whole, amazingly recent, despite the fact that speculations about man, his origins, his differences in customs and ideas, seem to be as old as human thought. From the 1500s through the 1700s, the voyages of "discoverers" made the then-literate world increasingly aware of other peoples and their ways. So different did the "Indians" of the New World seem to the *conquistadores*, for example, that it became necessary for the Pope to issue a bull in the 1500s for the purpose of stating that Indians are human beings and are entitled to be treated as such. Even as late as the eighteenth century, Carolus Linnaeus, the great natural history systematizer, was led by the then-current beliefs to include in his classification of man not only *Homo sapiens* ("thinking man"), but also *Homo ferus* ("wild man"), and *Homo monstrosus* ("man monster"). Only very gradually did the strange creatures and mythical lands portrayed in current tales and travelers' legends become discredited and relegated to limbo. Alexander von Humboldt explored the Orinoco River region in the early nineteenth century, dispelling the myth that the Indians there had mouths where their navels should be. But some mistaken notions lingered on, occasionally fostered by the managers of carnivals and sideshows who displayed a "wild man from Borneo" (who often bore little resemblance to anyone from that country).

By the early 1800s, however, the habit of precise observation was better established. Rumors and myths had been and were being checked up on. Large reservoirs of information about man and his nature—physical and cultural—were being collected. Two important things came from this period: awareness of others who shared the fact of being human, and an awakening concern for those human creatures who were being exploited by their fellow man. As people became increasingly aware of the predicament of the Tasmanians who were being shot down, of the treatment given black slaves in the Americas and elsewhere, and so on, they began to form humanitarian organizations to fight for their protection. It was in these same times and on the basis of some of these same concerns that the first anthropological and ethnological societies and journals came into being.

During this same period in the United States, where the great Indian wars were just ending and the frontiers were rapidly vanishing, there came to be great popular interest in some American Indians, especially in those chiefs or warriors who had achieved notice in some way. "This interest was, of course, of a romantic or sentimental kind and manifested itself mostly in written accounts of the 'noble savage,' the 'vanishing red man,' and similar tales" [Langness 1965, p. 5]. In 1832 B. B. Thatcher published *Indian Biography: or, An Historical Account of Those Individuals Who Have Been Distinguished Among the North American Natives as Orators, Warriors, Statesmen and Other Remarkable Characters*. Artists and travellers began to supplement their Indian studies with brief biographies. In the later 1800s there appeared a series called *Famous American Indians*, and individual biographies of such famous Indians as Sitting Bull [1891], Black Hawk of the Sauk [1854], Pontiac of the Ottawa [1861], Brant of the Mohawk [1865], Chief Joseph of the Nez Percé [1881], Uncas of the Mohicans [1842], and Sequoya of the Cherokee [1885], to name a few [Langness 1965, p. 5].

L. L. Langness, author of *The Life History in Anthropological Science* [1965], mentions various other biographies of Indians in the early 1900s, which he groups with those mentioned above as "popular accounts." In summary he states, however, that "no real interest in biography as a specific tool for research had been shown by anthropologists" until the 1920s when Paul Radin published his famous *Crashing Thunder*. In making this statement, he does not choose to consider several brief biographical sketches by Grinnell, Kroeber, Wallis and others. Clyde Kluckhohn [1945] had previously called attention to the lack of anthropological use of the life history, and to the fact that any potential the early popular accounts possessed as sources of data had never been exploited by anthropologists.

Langness considers all of the other kinds of data with which anthropologists characteristically return from the field and questions whether they alone can be an adequate substitute for an intensive life history. He concludes that while life histories were not considered truly mandatory in most anthropological studies fifty years ago, they have been becoming increasingly important ever since, especially in certain types of studies, such as those which emphasize personality and culture, the role of the individual in society, or developmental history. From the 1920s, then, there was some increase in attention being focused on the individual in society—not only in the United States but in Europe as well, especially in Germany. In the United States, the focus in the first anthropological life histories, still called autobiographies by many of their collectors, continued to be on American Indians. In the 1930s Truman Michelson collected the "autobiographies" of three Indian women from different tribes—of special importance because they were early attempts to present the female side of what has remained a heavily male-oriented subject [Langness 1965, p. 7].

Looking back at the life histories that have been collected, Langness credits Edward Sapir and Paul Radin with having made the greatest and most enduring contributions to the field. He credits Sapir with having bridged the disciplines of psychology and psychiatry, as well as anthropology, greatly affecting the "school" of personality and culture, and influencing the work of Ruth Benedict, Ernest Beaglehole, and Walter Dyk [1965, p. 8]. From Pelto's quotation given earlier, it can be seen that Radin's interest in life history materials was of a very different sort.

Although many scholars were engaged in work with American Indians on reservations and elsewhere in the period between 1925 and 1945, most were oriented toward the idea that Indian cultures were fast disappearing and it was essential to salvage as much of them as possible. Life histories were not usually seen as a necessary part of the job, perhaps partly because they are more time-consuming than many other methods of data collection. At any rate, the bulk of anthropological biography during the period was directed toward "clarifying or portraying the cultural dimension of human existence rather than the idiosyncratic or psychological dimension" [Langness 1965, p. 9]. Among the most interesting and valuable studies of the period are Dyk's *Son of Old Man Hat* [1938], Ford's *Smoke from Their Fires* [1941], and Leo Simmons' *Sun Chief* [1942], as well as Radin's *Crashing Thunder*, mentioned earlier.

Langness summarizes the 1925–1945 period as showing an increasing interest in life histories and in the methodology of life-history collection. He notes that since 1945 there has been a growing trend toward "less difficult methods of gathering data" [1965, p. 19]. The life histories of the post-1945 period have, however, shown far greater diversity in the people chosen as subjects, as well as in the approaches utilized. The requests of many social scientists for greater numbers of carefully documented life histories still remain inadequately answered. The major inadequacies, aside from sheer numbers, include frequent lack of documentation to explain and give the setting for the study; very uneven representation of age and sex groups, with males over fifty as the vast majority of subjects; little contextual material and few life histories from the same group, hence little opportunity for comparison or judging how representative a particular life history is; and lack of analysis and interpretation.

Unlike the situation with so many other aspects of fieldwork, there simply is no good "how to" book about the collection of life histories. This is part of the reason why we have quoted rather extensively from some of the few published sources, so that you may refer to them for suggestions if you like. Although it is now nearly thirty years old, we feel that the section by Kluckhohn in *The Use of Personal Documents in History, Anthropology, and Sociology* [1945], especially the section on "Field Techniques and Methods," contains more useful information and suggestions than any other source on the subject. Many of the thoughts that follow have some basis in his suggestions.

A primary suggestion is that the collector of a life history should not depend solely upon reading about the community in question before starting his interviews with a life-history informant. To select informants carefully and probably to establish sufficient rapport with them, the fieldworker should get a "feel" of the community from first-hand observation. The precise steps taken to do this will vary from place to place and with various situations. When one does not know a community well, it is also easy, as we mentioned earlier, to blunder into "touchy" topics or things that would be considered too personal and private if one does not know the area well. Often, too, a bonus can come from beginning in an impersonal field and looking at the whole community because the informant may then relax and feel more confident since he does not feel that the whole focus of attention is on him alone. In your research for this project, it would be ideal if you were invited to visit in the informant's home. If such an invitation is not freely forthcoming on short acquaintance, perhaps you will be able to visit the informant at his or her work site, favorite sunny park bench, or another place where the informant will feel "at home," and you may be able to meet, or at least see, the informant's friends and acquaintances as he or she interacts with them. Wherever and whenever you visit your informant, always be sure that your presence is expected, not unwelcome, and not a hindrance to any other activity in which the informant is engaged.

The question of motivating the informant can become a difficult problem, as Kluckhohn reports from experience [p. 117], unless there is something about which the informant would like to let off steam or something about his life of which he is particularly proud. This is, of course, especially true if one wants to collect the whole of a lengthy and complicated tale and the informant is a busy person. Many people also consciously or unconsciously resent being "pumped dry" [Kluckhohn, p. 118], hence it is a good idea to "prime the pump" by telling stories of one's own life, thus giving a feeling of sharing. In many situations, especially where the informant is an old acquaintance, it may be sufficient to ask something like, "Won't you help me out with my work?" In other cases, the desire to help someone really know the truth about the community instead of "some of the lies about us in books" may be a strong motivating factor.

One thing that Kluckhohn emphasizes has particular relevance for the rather time-consuming business of gathering a life history. He points out that even if a particular person is a very desirable potential informant from the point of view of sampling, of articulateness, and of many other factors we have mentioned, he is usually "a bad risk if the inevitable pressures upon him to engage in other activities are strong and likely to be cumulative" [pp. 120–121]. If such a person has agreed to be a life-history informant only to be helpful and friendly, but against his better judgment or that of influential family members, he may well have to cut short the interview, or may hurriedly telescope episodes so that they become lifeless and uninteresting. Kluckhohn also warns that the person who is "capricious or unstable or characterized by highly ephemeral enthusiasms" should be avoided unless he is especially needed as an informant [p. 121]. The difficulties of detecting such qualities of temperament on short acquaintance are, of course, great, but the fieldworker should attempt to evaluate the nature and intensity of the motivation of his subjects.

Kluckhohn suggests that certain aspects of the situation can be carefully structured by the investigator, with one eye on cultural conditions and the other on the informant's personality and motivations. Sometimes a third eye might be very useful! We mentioned earlier that if it is agreeable to the informant and in no way troublesome to him, it is good to conduct an interview in a place where he is, or at least feels, at home, and where one can see him in interaction with others. This is partly because it is very good to get an idea of the context of the informant's life and to add to one's knowledge, if possible, by speaking with others about things which concern the informant. There are, however, difficulties in controlling all of the factors involved. A friend of ours, who had established good rapport with a married couple over a considerable period, asked the husband, who had always been a particularly willing, insightful, and articulate informant, to tell him his life story. When he arrived at the home at the appointed hour, he was greeted at the door by the wife, who kindly ushered him in but, as they sat down to talk, said, "I don't know what you want to interview him for. He's never done anything worth writing about. You should interview somebody who's had an interesting life!" This was undoubtedly meant as a show of modesty, but it effectively convinced the husband that he knew nothing worth saying. The interview was quickly completed; and the husband later reluctantly denied permission for it to be published in a group of life histories. Similar occurrences are frequent enough so that you should be on the lookout to prevent them. It might be necessary, for example, to conduct interviews in your own headquarters in the community if such a problem threatens.

Although some aspects of life history interviewing are not clearly formulated and spelled out, there is one aspect about which everyone who has done extensive and useful life-history interviewing is sure: the need to remain at times a kind of "blank screen upon which the informant projects his life"

[Kluckhohn, p. 122]. The ethnographer should be as nondirective as possible; and, once the informant understands the task ahead, the ethnographer should say as little as possible, never interrupting unless the house is on fire! To interrupt is to discourage; and the topic in question will probably never be returned to as satisfactorily. The ethnographer must be sensitive to the informant's reactions, but should usually speak only to reassure or break a complete silence. It is, of course, exceedingly difficult to be both a blank screen and a friend, but this kind of approach may be necessary for the free flow of personal statement and the maintenance of essential support.

In life-history interviews the subject matter is somewhat personal, and the relationship between ethnographer and informant is never cursory and simple as when some other information is gathered in the field. These are additional reasons why informants for life-history research should be chosen with special care. Kluckhohn speaks [p. 122] of the necessity for the anthropologist to build up a trust comparable to that enjoyed by a physician, lawyer, or priest, and to honor in every way the obligations involved. This is no small challenge, and must be taken seriously. The ethical responsibility for protecting the informant and his anonymity is of great importance, especially now that members of the community being studied are likely to read about themselves. It is important to try to get informants to agree to publication of their lives and to get others who will be affected also to agree to publication of what is being said about them. It is also coming to be true that publishers are reluctant to put out any life history for which permission has not been given by the informant—in writing, if possible.

Another important matter that Kluckhohn brings up is that of recording and keeping a verbatim record without stopping the informant—since rapport is almost always damaged unless the subject can select and maintain his own tempo [p. 127]. Stenography or some forms of speedwriting are solutions he suggests, although today's mechanized anthropologist would also suggest a tape recorder. The length of an interview must be worked out carefully, since some informants tire quickly while others hate to break off.

When collecting life history material, one should always try to get as much information as possible from people other than the informant. In this way, one can pick up differences between the informant's conception of himself and others' conceptions of him. It also serves as a check for information that the informant would be reluctant to give or has given incorrectly. It is also worthwhile, if possible, to obtain accounts by other eyewitnesses to events recounted in detail by the informant.

THE PROJECT

Collect the life history of an informant, bearing in mind the several suggestions from Kluckhohn. This is to be a nondirective interview, so that it is, as much as possible, the informant's own story in every way, emphasizing what he himself thinks it is important to tell rather than what the questioner thinks it is important to ask about. Thus, as soon as you are sure the informant understands what is wanted, you can begin with such nondirective questions as, "Please tell me about your life as a child," or "What was it like to grow up here in Blankville at the turn of the century?" (Despite their nondirective nature, such questions may well have been planned in advance.) This kind of interviewing may be useful for most of the collection of a life history with voluble and insightful informants. In most cases, however, other kinds of more directive, specific questions are necessary as well. Please remember Kluckhohn's very important caution against interrupting your informant unless it is absolutely necessary to do so.

If the life history is collected in more than one session, it is a good idea to think out questions raised by the first session and to ask them of the informant in the next interview session, or in a brief visit for final questions. With informants who can manage to think through a chronology, it is wise to work out a year-by-year list of events as a check for the ordering of the items in the history.

When you write up and present your material, please remember all of the necessary ethical safeguards for your informant, including the possible necessity of giving him or her a fictitious name, or otherwise hiding him or her, unless you have full permission to use the real name and all of the details in your story.

SELECTED ANNOTATED BIBLIOGRAPHY

Casagrande, Joseph B., ed.
   In the Company of Man: Twenty Portraits of Anthropological Informants. Harper, 1960. The twenty life histories recorded by well-known anthropologists

are fascinating reading in themselves, and also give insights into the ethnographer-informant relationship in producing a life history.

Dyk, Walter

> *Son of Old Man Hat: A Navaho Autobiography.* Harcourt, 1938. Lively, fascinating reading. Thoroughly recommended.

Ford, Clellan S.

> *Smoke from Their Fires.* Yale University Press, 1941. Also an interesting account.

Kluckhohn, Clyde

> "The Personal Document in Anthropological Science." In L. Gottschalk, C. Kluckhohn, and R. Angell, eds., *The Use of Personal Documents in History, Anthropology, and Sociology.* Social Science Research Council, 1945, Bulletin 53:78–173. Although thirty years old, this is still a valuable and helpful collection of ideas and suggestions.

Langness, L. L.

> *The Life History in Anthropological Science.* Holt, Rinehart and Winston, 1965. A good little manual on the uses of life-history material. Ample bibliographic treatment.

Mandelbaum, David G.

> "The Study of Life History: Gandhi." *Current Anthropology* 1973, 14, (3):177–196. A recent review of life-history research, with additional suggestions on reading life histories based upon literature rather than interviews.

Mead, Margaret

> *Coming of Age in Samoa.* William Morrow, 1928.

Mead, Margaret

> *Growing Up in New Guinea.* William Morrow, 1930. Two of Mead's pioneering works, both emphasizing children and adolescents.

Pelto, Pertti J.

> *Anthropological Research: The Structure of Inquiry.* Harper & Row, 1970. A carefully prepared treatment on a great many types of anthropological research—little treatment is actually given to life histories.

Radin, Paul

> *The Autobiography of a Winnebago Indian.* University of California Publications in American Archaeology and Ethnology, 1920, 16:381–473. Subsequently published as *Crashing Thunder.* Still good reading.

Simmons, Leo W.

> *Sun Chief, The Autobiography of a Hopi Indian.* Yale University Press, 1942. Probably ranks with *Son of Old Man Hat* as one of the most fascinating to read.

Van Gennep, Arnold

> *Les Rites de Passage.* Paris: Libraire Cortique, Emile Nouray, 1900. The classic work on puberty ceremonies.

PROJECT SEVEN

USING PERSONAL DOCUMENTATION

INTRODUCTION

An anthropologist in the field ordinarily gathers much of his information through observation and by some form of direct interviewing. In some cases, however, it is not feasible for him to interview everyone. For example, he might be working in a very large village and, although he has met everyone at least once in the course of taking a census, he might have to make the most efficient use of his time by concentrating on only a few key informants.

If he is working in a literate community, he can sometimes collect personal documentation. To be sure, any time an informant tells anything to the anthropologist the latter is collecting "personal documentation"; but, for the purposes of this chapter, we can restrict that term and apply it mainly to extended narrative accounts. By far the most commonly used form of personal documentation is the life history, described in Project 6. The life history is most frequently collected by the interviewer in person. A less commonly used approach is the collection of diaries or autobiographical essays. Such a method has the advantage of providing the anthropologist with information from a wider circle of people than he might otherwise be able to work with in person in an ongoing way.

Most of the anthropologists who have made use of this technique have tended to rely on some existing group, such as secondary-school students, for whom the writing of an essay might be considered part of the normal course of events. In many communities, adults are not accustomed to writing more than an occasional letter, and might feel threatened by the request to write something fairly elaborate. A possible means of overcoming such reluctance might be to ask the adults to keep running diaries of brief jottings, rather than to write full-blown prose narratives. Such diaries have been used extensively by psychologists dealing with individual case histories, but they can also be employed profitably by anthropologists studying group activity. Essays and diaries can be used to elicit information on a wide variety of subjects. Essentially any topic that could be the subject of a personal interview could also be written down by a literate informant.

There are two main categories of information for which such a technique seems particularly appropriate. When one is interested in outlining the daily round of activities, the diaries of informants (whether they are in more or less constant contact with the fieldworker, or are somewhat peripheral to his circle of key informants) can provide a picture of the mundane events that fill the days of people in the community. Because a person will fill a diary with what he or she considers important, a study of informants' diaries can give us a very good indication of what people in a particular culture feel to be significant in the world around them—as opposed to what the analyst perceives to be important on the basis of his outsider's perspective. By comparing several of these, the anthropologist can make some fairly definitive statements about what constitutes the typical lifestyle. He does this not merely to catalog mundane events but also to round out his understanding of the life cycle among the people he is studying.

On the other hand, the fieldworker is often especially interested in eliciting statements on values and attitudes. In the American school of cultural anthropology the study of shared values receives important emphasis; and, indeed, most commonly held definitions of "culture" include some indication of the value system of the people, in addition to the things that they make, do, or create. Individuals, of course, will value different things, and hold different opinions on a variety of issues, but there are certain attitudes that are more or less common to the members of a given society. These are the attitudes that help to hold that society together, because they represent areas in which a diversity of individual interests can come together in agreement.

In anthropological literature one finds a bewildering array of terms—"sentiments," "values," "patterns," "themes," "premises," and so on — that refer to constellations of shared ideas and attitudes. We need not become involved in definitional problems because, for the purposes of this project, all these related concepts can be spoken of in Ralph Linton's phrase as "anything which has meaning for two or more of society's component members" [Linton 1956, p. 422].

A society stays together only as long as its members are in some sort of general agreement as to what they are doing and what they are striving toward.

> A stable social structure prevails only so long as the majority of individuals in the society find enough satisfaction both in the goals socially approved and in the institutionalized means of attainment to compensate them for the constraints which ordered social life inevitably imposes upon uninhibited response to impulse. In any way of life there is much that to an outside observer appears haphazard, disorderly, more or less chaotic. But unless most participants feel that the ends and means of their culture make sense, disorientation and amorality become rampant [Kluckhohn & Leighton 1961, pp. 295–296].

One way an anthropologist can better understand the areas of agreement that hold any particular society together is to see how often statements of such values turn up in the discourse of the people, and then to see in what contexts they turn up. But, since people do not always verbalize the values by which they guide their lives, it is often charged that anthropologists are too vague when they deal in the realm of values and attitudes. Getting informants to verbalize their attitudes, then, is one of the reasons for the use of the personal documentation technique.

An example of the use of personal documentation concerns the island of Saba, a tiny island in the northern part of the Lesser Antilles (the long arc of islands in the Caribbean), which is politically affiliated with the Netherlands. Saba is essentially a single steep volcanic peak. Until recent years there has been no way for ships to land there because of the pounding surf and the lack of protected harbors. Even air service was impossible until almost a decade ago because of the lack of level landing space. As a result, Saba people characteristically emigrated if they chose to pursue the economic and social benefits offered by the world outside. "The young people of Saba believe it is good to emigrate," one ethnographer may say. But how do we know? Obviously, a survey questionnaire would take us only so far. For example, an ethnographer asked young people in Saba the question: "Would you like to live the main part of your life in Saba or some other country?" The statement could then be revised to say, "All but one of the forty-five respondents over twelve years of age said that they would prefer to spend the main parts of their lives in some other place" [Crane 1971, p. 197]. But, even so, we would know very little about why young people plan to leave or what this orientation to emigration means to the society. But a collection of short autobiographies written by schoolchildren gives a clear picture of how deeply the idea of emigration is rooted in the culture. Moreover, by examining the contexts in which emigration is mentioned in the autobiographies we can learn more about why people plan for and expect it. Because the statements are in their own words, we can get some of the feeling tone surrounding emigration as well. Four young people wrote as follows:

> I'd like to go America to school because I have family there. Because when you become a woman there isn't any work here for anybody to do. So if you want to earn money the best thing is to go away and earn a living or if you're still young to go to school until you're old enough. Because your father and mother do not live forever. And they will not be here to support you.

> I would not like to stay on Saba. Because there is no future for boys and girls. I want to go to Aruba. Where I can finish school. On Saba you can't go nowhere. Sometimes swimming on a Sunday, or to the movies. But I seldom go.

> I don't want to remain always on Saba. I want to go to Aruba or Curacao. I don't want to stay here because all you can do is to work in the ground or keep cattle.

> I do not want to remain always in Saba. Well you see Saba is small and doesn have nothing to interest you and after you have been in a place so long you don't find it so interrested. Well I can't say where I want to go, because there are so many places I want to go but when you are poor you can't do any better. So that is all [Crane 1971, pp. 198–199].

It is a well-known anthropological truism that behaviors that appear similar occur in many parts of the world, but the connotations and implications of those behaviors may vary widely. An example of this concerns a study undertaken in five communities in the Southwest among Zuñi and Navajo Indians, Spanish-Americans, Texas homesteaders, and Mormons [Kluckhohn Strodtbeck 1961]. All five communities were within several miles of one another and had to cope with the same ecological problems. Yet, because of the distinct value systems on the basis of which the groups were operating, each community came up with different "answers" to the same sorts of problems. Farming, for example, meant a link to the past and to the ancestors as far as the Zuñi were concerned. For the Texas homesteaders it meant a stake in the future and a break with the Dust Bowl hardships of the past. Thus, the same activity has two separate meanings, depending on the cultural context in which it occurs. Personal documentation analysis can sort out the contextual meaning of such behaviors and establish the cultural dimensions of a particular value or attitude. Moreover, the anthropologist can compare what people say they think and do, or plan to do, with their actual behavior. This may help the anthropologist to some insights into differences between ideal culture and real culture.

Ordinarily, the source of the anthropologist's assertion that "the young people of Saba believe it is good to emigrate" is his knowledge of the community; presumably, numerous people whose reputations for honesty and reliability are not in doubt have told him so repeatedly in different settings. But if it is possible for the fieldworker to have those same sentiments written down by the informants themselves, he can more easily quantify his statement. In addition, he can use the exact words of his informants for illustrative purposes, a very important consideration when preparing a full ethnographic report from one's field research. Obviously, personal documentation is not the only source of such information. Some fieldworkers have had success in providing informants with cameras and asking them to take pictures of "good things" or "important people." Such a method, however, is not always practical in terms of budgetary considerations. Other anthropologists prefer to cross-check value statements by use of the standard psychological projective tests like the Rorschach and Thematic Apperception Test. But, as these require a great deal of specialized study to administer and interpret, the fieldworker should not rely on them unless he himself has mastered the special techniques or has access to a psychologist colleague who is willing to aid in the analysis.

The British anthropologist John Beattie, who has made extensive use of personal documentation, feels that obtaining " . . . written statements either dictated by the informant to the anthropologist or his assistant and written down by him verbatim, or written down directly by the informant himself, is a vitally important part of modern fieldwork" [Beattie 1965, p. 30]. Indeed, his ethnography of the Bunyoro Kingdom in East Africa is studded with such personal accounts, giving it a very personalized flavor. One of Beattie's interesting innovations was to organize two essay competitions, not only for schoolchildren but for all the literate members of the community. The Nyoro people, he found, had a flair for describing their culture — particularly its more esoteric aspects, such as sorcery and spirit mediumship — in prose form, although they ordinarily do not write such things down. As a result, he learned a great deal about Bunyoro society that he might never have uncovered through verbal interviews.

Beattie sent a circular letter to the various locations where the people were living, explaining that he had come to their country to learn the "rules and customs of Bunyoro-Kitara both of long ago and those of today" [Beattie 1965, p. 31]. He invited all interested people to write what they knew about certain topics which he outlined in his letter. Cash prizes were offered for the best essays, as an added incentive.

In general, Beattie called for topics that he knew to be important in the culture, but about which he lacked information. He also called for a "residual" category, to allow people to write on other topics that they felt were important and that he might not have thought of himself. In the second competition, begun toward the end of his field study, he asked more focused questions and called for essays on topics for which he required certain specific data. [See Beattie 1965, pp. 30–37].

Vera Rubin and Marisa Zavalloni [1969] set out to study the attitudes of children in what is often called a "Third World" country. Everyone talks about the impact of modernization in the "Third World," and most people agree that it is the educated youth of those areas who feel that impact with the greatest force. The Rubin-Zavalloni study, set on the island of Trinidad in the West Indies, concentrated primarily on survey questionnaires, to sort out aspects of the modernization experience as they affected the young people of the island. But one of the administered questions elicited essays that yielded some very dramatic illustrations of the meaning these processes hold for the adolescents involved. The young people were asked to write about their plans, expectations, and hopes beginning at the present and going up to the year 2000. The students were told that if they did not wish to write their own "future autobiographies" they could write for imaginary subjects of their own age and position [p. 210]. One brief example:

> My family has a little plot of sugar cane which does not yield as before because the strength of the land is failing and the scientific methods which they have is too expensive, because he has a very little holding. I can then try to help my village as a whole, for it is a little one, but it has much potential and future. I can try and see that any factories or plants be opened up in my little village where the younger men would be able to get good jobs, and the little village could be made a very good one for any one to live in. If I become an influential man I can try to have any colleges or institutes not far from my area, so that it would be cheaper for the poor village peasants to get in their children without much trouble and expense [p. 165].

The frequency with which similar themes of economic development as the key to all kinds of happiness (including the benefits of education and political "influence") recur seems to indicate that the children see the growing disparity between the new, modernized elite (who are involved in the incipient industries of the island) and the old rural peasantry as the most troublesome aspect of culture change. This statement, general though it is, is certainly a far stronger one than the simple assertion that "children in the Third World are troubled by modernization and feel alienated."

On Trinidad's sister island, Tobago, a young Englishman named Chris Searle learned an important anthropological lesson by using something of the same tactic. He was faced with the contradictions of a situation in which he, a white man, was teaching black children about "their" heritage – actually the heritage of the colonialists – and he was concerned lest he impose too much of his own experience on them, and thereby fail to encourage them to realize what was unique in their own social and cultural heritage. Therefore, he began to collect samples of written work from his students, since in writing the children were less shy about revealing themselves than they might have been in spoken discourse. Searle then analyzed these stories and poems in order to find out what the dominant themes in these children's lives were, in order to understand their own particular "world view" better.

For one small example, Searle tackled the theme of the "island." In the minds of Europeans or Americans, the island has traditionally symbolized escape, romance, glamour, adventure.

But for the black children, whose ancestors had been **brought to** the "island paradise" in chains, and who see it as an increasingly inconsequential dot on the map of the great, white world beyond, Tobago often connotes a place of isolation and imprisonment. The children feel that they are all "forsaken," and must accept the "guilt" for the "aloneness and forsakenness of the black children in the white world."

> Advantages of living on an island are, in an island their [sic] will not be much violence, discrimination as in the countries. In an island the people there will have to work hard at their jobs whether it is working in a garden or in a store.
>
> Most of the people there will be hard working people and when they work for a few cents, all will spend to feed and clothe a family. Rich people will not mistreat their servants. If someone is working for some one they will be treated kindly.
>
> In an island there will be peace and hardly any noise. The most noise you may here [sic] is from the animals playing in bushes. There will not be many kidnapping many road deaths and sad scenes.
>
> Children who live on an island will be healthy, cheerful children, they will be contented and grow up obedient and hard working in both work and schooling.
>
> On some island there will be lovely beaches with palm trees and coconut trees. Most of the trees and shrubs will be there and an artist could make a good scenery there. Tourism will go on on an island because there will be quietness, and peace and thats what tourist likes. They also come to see the beautiful flowers in bloom.
>
> People will be welcome with hospitality on an island more than in a city. There will be pleasant smiles and friendly and cheerful greetings as they pass you. They won't be much haughtiness and quarrels about who has more money . . . [Searle 1972, pp. 16–17].*

Despite the chins-up attitude of the thirteen-year-old authoress, she already knows that the quietness and flowers are for the tourist and the hard work is for the natives; the best the latter can hope for is to be "treated kindly" as servants. Tobago is billed as "Robinson Crusoe's isle," and is fast becoming a tourist mecca, which seems destined to make peace and quiet even harder to find, and to alienate the island's inhabitants even more from their homeland.

---

*From *The Forsaken Lover: White Words and Black People* by Chris Searle, pp. 16–17. Reprinted by permission of Routledge & Kegan Paul Ltd.

THE PROJECT

Your project is to analyze a body of personal documents for clues to the sociocultural setting of which they are a part. For convenience, you should select a relatively small group of no more than ten individuals as your sample population. This will, of course, restrict the number of generalizations you can legitimately make from the data, but it should be sufficient to enable you to see what sorts of inferences can be made.

If you have access to a school class (primary or secondary), this might be a logical place to start. However, you can select the ten individuals at random as long as they are linked in some way that might lead you to believe they would be able to express ideas about a common topic. Ten people who happen to get on a bus at the same time would not be a suitable group. Members of a college class, of a political or social club, or a religious congregation, or an ethnic or racial group might all be possible subjects. If your instructor agrees, you can, of course, combine this project with one or more of the others; for example, you can use the same congregation members who are your subjects in the Participant Observation project.

Your directions to these individuals should be rather general. The technique of asking them to write their autobiographies through the year 2000 is effective if you are dealing with adolescents, although it could be depressing or offensive to older people. A neutral topic, then, might be suggested, such as "Life in Our Town," "Trends in Campus Life," or "What Our Church Is Like." The topic should be something that the informants are reasonably interested in and about which they have something to say, and it should be open enough to allow them to speak freely about what is really on their minds. Be sure that you explain to the informants that their names will not be used in anything you write about your study and that you are not concerned about such things as grammar and spelling. Encourage them to be frank.

You may, if you have extra time, ask for a second series of essays, on more specific topics—topics that may have been suggested by questions raised by the general essays the first time around. In any case, once you have your collection of texts, you can analyze them much as you would any other textual material, such as folklore. You should be primarily concerned with the recurring themes of these essays, since these are likely to define the areas of "common interest" within the group. Your information will probably fall into two broad categories:

- specific information (data on "the culture")

- statements of ideas and attitudes, reflecting the way people respond to those "facts of life"

What are the points of agreement between the two in the individual essays? What are the themes that run through most or all of the essays? Most important, what is the "cultural meaning" behind the various facts of the culture — for example, how do the informants feel about doing a certain thing?

SELECTED ANNOTATED BIBLIOGRAPHY

Beattie, John
    Bunyoro: An African Kingdom. Holt, Rinehart and Winston, 1960. Beattie's ethnography, which depends in part on the use of personal documentation.
Beattie, John
    Understanding an African Kingdom: Bunyoro. Holt, Rinehart and Winston, 1965. An interesting account of how one anthropologist went about his fieldwork; includes some valuable information on the use of documentation.
Crane, Julia G.
    Educated to Emigrate: The Social Organization of Saba. Assen, Netherlands: Royal van Gorcum, 1971. The ethnography of a Caribbean island which includes the use of personal documentation.
Kluckhohn, Clyde
    "The Personal Document in Anthropological Science." In L. Gottschalk, C. Kluckhohn, and R. Angell, eds., *The Use of Personal Documents in History, Anthropology, and Sociology.* Social Science Research Council, 1945, Bulletin 53:78–173.
Kluckhohn, Clyde, and others
    "Values and Value Orientations in the Theory of Action: An Exploration in Definition and Classification." In T. Parsons and E. Shils, eds., *Toward a General Theory of Action.* Harper & Row, 1962. This is an often cited example of the anthropological usage of the concepts dealt with in this project.
Kluckhohn, Clyde, and Dorothea Leighton
    The Navaho. Natural History Library (Doubleday), rev. ed., 1962.
Kluckhohn, Florence, Fred. L. Strodtbeck, et al.
    Variation in Value Orientations. Row, Peterson, 1961. A comparative study of values in five Southwestern communities.
Leighton, Alexander H.
    My Name is Legion. Basic Books, 1959. Appendix A [pp. 395–420] is a comprehensive review of the concepts of sentiment, value, etc., as used in the various social sciences, including anthropology. The accompanying bibliography is excellent, particularly for some of the older, less commonly used sources.

Linton, Ralph

> *The Study of Man.* Appleton-Century-Crofts, 1936. A classic introduction to anthropology; many of Linton's definitions — as of "value" and "interest" in this project, or of "status" and "role" — have become standard among American anthropologists.

Rubin, Vera, and Marisa Zavalloni

> *We Wish to Be Looked Upon: A Study of the Aspirations of Youth in a Developing Society.* Teachers College Press, 1969. An exhaustive survey of the attitudes of school children on the island of Trinidad. The appendices contain the survey questionnaires and essay instructions used to glean these data on values and attitudes.

Searle, Chris

> *The Forsaken Lover: White Words and Black People.* London: Routledge and Kegan Paul, 1972. A young Englishman, a teacher in a school on the West Indian island of Tobago, learned about the "values and attitudes" of his students through their essays and poems, which he collected and interpreted in this volume.

PROJECT EIGHT

DIGGING INTO CULTURAL HISTORY

INTRODUCTION

Anthropology includes within its scope an emphasis upon the history of man's development. Clearly, historical research can provide important insights for understanding culture. A culture is to a great extent conditioned by what it has been, and it is not possible to understand fully what is occurring in the present, or why it is occurring, without reference to the past. In fact, the British anthropologist R. R. Marrett once declared that "anthropology is history or it is nothing."

The fact that we now have a much fuller picture of the past is in large measure a result of anthropological research. Anthropologists do differ, however, in the degree to which they value the historical perspective. Some social anthropologists, for example, concentrate almost entirely on comparing cultures existing at the same time. Nevertheless, contributions to understanding the past come from all four major subdivisions of the discipline. The ethnographer, the kind of anthropologist on whose work we are concentrating most in this volume, characteristically gives time depth and a broader perspective to his work by interviewing people of all ages about their lives, by gathering these people's recollections of the lives of their ancestors, by studying any documents that may be available locally or in centralized archives, and so on.

Archaeologists are, of course, especially committed to the discovery of man's past. The word archaeology comes from the Greek and means, literally, "the study of old things." It involves the recovery, study, and reconstruction of the past of man—processes that must be carried out both scientifically and imaginatively. Anthropological archaeologists have characteristically interested themselves in digging up and interpreting the material remains of culture from the vast periods of the past for which there is no written history. Recently, however, many of them, particularly in the United States, have worked on historic sites as well as those representing prehistoric periods.

It is often possible to gain experience in archaeology by taking part in an authentic excavation (a "dig") or by working in the laboratory with artifacts found in the field. Skill in archaeological fieldwork comes mostly from doing it, not from reading about it. A very important caution to insert here is that if you are aware of a place where, for example, arrowheads or pieces of Indian pottery are being found, it should be reported to your state archaeologist. To dig a site is to destroy it, so the only people who should ever conduct a dig are those well trained in archaeological techniques. Only trained archaeologists can create, as they dig, all of the meticulous records that preserve knowledge of how the earth and the materials it contained were arranged in relationship to one another. When a treasure-hunter finds something that interests him and takes it from the earth, he is ignoring its context. All of the earth and objects around his artifact, and the way those artifacts are associated with one another, could provide the clues an archaeologist needs to determine its date and its function in the former society. A great deal of effort has gone into developing systematic techniques for preserving more and more material remains from sites, and for recording more exactly the positions of objects and features found in a dig. Obviously, fishhooks, seed baskets, and arrowheads can reveal something about how a people made their living. But one or two of each can tell little of a culture. It is only when the archaeologist knows, for example, that there were once many fishhooks and few arrowheads in use by the people of an area, and that later there were many arrowheads and few fishhooks, that he can say hunting was becoming comparatively more important in the local economy and fishing less so. It is the context that provides the information the archaeologist must have to reconstruct a culture. Of course, his later conclusions about an ancient culture depend upon his performing a careful and scientific excavation. He may be aided in his analysis by scientists in other fields, such as botanists and zoologists, whose specialized knowledge of plants, pollen, horns, shells, bone, and so forth can be essential in rounding out the total picture.

Some texts speak of archaeologists as the "glamour boys of anthropology." To the extent that this is true, it is partly because the people being studied are forever beyond our reach, so that the archaeologist must bring considerable knowledge and skill to his work—as well as the less glamourous trait, self-discipline. Like a detective, the archaeologist wants to learn about people and their behavior; yet the only clues to the people he studies may well exist solely in hidden objects and the marks in the soil that he is able to discover and analyze. Unfortunately, the passage of time and the ravaging effects of changing climate constantly destroy remains. The substances most resistant to decay are stone, metal, and pottery. Organic substances like shell, bone, antler, and wood are much more susceptible to decay. The poorest environment for preservation of organic material is the hot, moist jungle, where archaeologists sometimes find that all traces of organic material have disappeared within only five years. Whatever the conditions of preservation, the archaeologist must work with what he can find. This is often a tantalizingly small portion of the original material remains [Gorenstein 1965, pp. 20–23].

While the archaeologist is interested in any valid evidence about the past of humankind, most of the evidence, as we have suggested, is to be found beneath the earth's surface. Stratigraphy, the observation of the earth's layers, or strata, and the principle of *superposition* are two important foundations for the study of the past. The use of stratigraphy in archaeology developed out of the pioneering work of geologists during the late eighteenth and early nineteenth centuries. (It is believed that Thomas Jefferson was the first person in the New World to conduct a dig which utilized these ideas.) One well-known British archaeologist has stated that the basis of scientific excavation is the carefully observed and accurately recorded stratigraphic profile.

Stratigraphy is based upon the simple principle that the upper layers of anything will have been placed there more recently than the lower layers. If, for example, you were to walk into a room and find that the baby of the family had piled his blocks one on top of the other, you would know that the upper blocks were placed on the pile after the lower blocks. Unless you had been watching the baby, however, you have no way of knowing how much later the upper blocks were added. This is an example of relative dating, because we know only that the placement of some blocks was relatively later in time than the placement of others. In archaeology, the principle of superposition is useful in that, unless the area has been very much disturbed, the digger can assume that, as he works his way down, each successively lower layer with the materials it contains will be older than the layers above. [See Figure 8–1.]

Although stratigraphic observation is only one of the principles that guide the archaeologist's trowel, we have chosen to mention it because of its basic importance in revealing sequences of prehistoric cultural changes. Under ideal conditions, sequences of evidence for cultural change may be found in clearly distinguishable layers at a stratified site. There are, however, many cases where conditions are far from ideal and no layering can be detected. In other cases, the materials we want to arrange in time sequence may not be found buried in the earth at all.

To ascertain cultural changes where stratigraphic evidence is unclear or lacking, archaeologists use *seriation*. Seriation is based on the idea that cultures change over time. By arranging something such as pottery or tomb types in sequences on the basis of degree of similarity, the archaeologist can arrive at a time sequence. The method was developed in 1902 by an Egyptologist who wanted to arrange a number of early tombs in time sequence. He worked out the sequence by studying the groups of pots placed with the skeletons. One particularly helpful clue was the nature of jar handles, which changed from useful extensions of the jars to more decorative handles, and later into mere painted lines.

As in jar handles, fashions come and go, which is obvious when we think of clothing styles, men's haircuts, high tailfins on automobiles, or crazes like hula hoops. Successions of technological advances in the historic periods of Western society have also followed one another in rather rapid succession, especially when seen in terms of the whole sweep of human development.

Figure 8-2 illustrates the changes in devices for artificial lighting that took place in Pennsylvania between 1850 and 1950. It is a clear example of an application of the seriation method. The succession of types seems obvious to us because we are somewhat aware of the history of such things. But an archaeologist working with pottery types may, at first, not know what the sequence of the types was like. Working out a sequence of types is only one step in seriation. The next step is to work out the frequency of each type of object at each site where it was found. As one type grows in popularity and forms a large proportion of the material culture, others decrease in frequency. When an archaeologist has worked out the pattern of increase and decrease of each type, he has the relative chronological position of

Figure 8–1

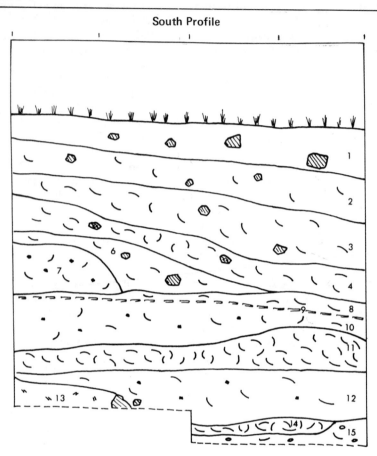

South Profile

1. Topsoil, plow zone
2. Transitional zone
3. Grey-brown loam/ash powder
4. Light brown compacted loam
5. Loose brown loam
6. Grey-brown compacted loam
7. Dark brown-black lens
8. Brown-black layer

SECTION DRAWINGS   SITE 1A, PIT 2

Source: From Donald L. Brockington, "Archaeological Investigations at Miahuatlan, Oaxaca," 1973, by permission of *Vanderbilt University Publications in Anthropology*. Drawn by Maria Jorrin.

Chart illustrating stratigraphic profiles of an archaeological site.

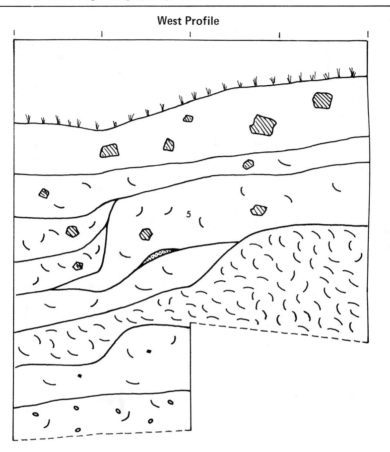

West Profile

9. Broken stucco floor

10. Light brown sandy loam

11. Light brown sandy loam with sherd concentration

12. Grey loam/ash with sherd concentration

13. Dark brown clay

14. Grey loam/ash powdered with sherd concentration

15. Compact sterile clay with limestone inclusions

Figure 8-2
Chart illustrating the seriation method

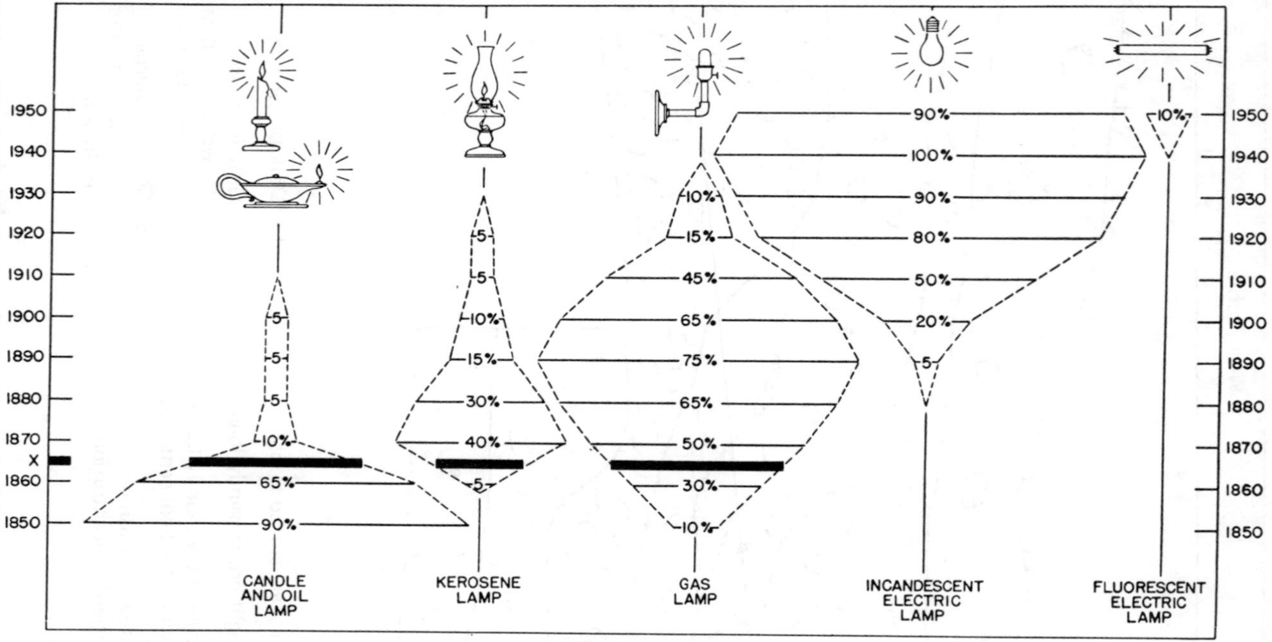

Source: From William J. Mayer-Oakes, *Prehistory of the Upper Ohio Valley*, 1955, by permission of the Carnegie Museum.

each of the sites from which his sample came. To use the lighting fixture example, for which we know the chronology, if a site in the Upper Ohio Valley yielded 80 per cent incandescent electric lamps, 10 per cent gas lamps, and 5 per cent kerosene lamps, it would suggest that the site was more recent than one that yielded a sample of 20 per cent incandescent electric lamps, 65 per cent gas lamps, and 10 per cent kerosene lamps.

For the archaeologist working with pottery types, the seriation method means arranging and rearranging the data on his various samples. The position of each sample on his chart represents its position in a time scale, so the archaeologist gradually develops the relative chronology of all of his sites [Gorenstein 1965, pp. 113 – 114].

Even if you cannot join a dig or work with a collection of material from one, you can use published evidence to carry on research into culture history. Kroeber and Richardson [1940], for example, once carefully analyzed style variations in European women's clothing for a three-hundred year period. They found that styles seem to be influenced by factors about which people are not even aware and that style changes occur in cycles, despite the efforts of designers and manufacturers. Not only did dress dimensions in general fluctuate in an orderly fashion, but each of the specific measures, such as waist height or fullness of skirt, had its own periodicity. As each dimension became more and more unlike the most characteristic form of that dimension, the probability that it would reverse directions increased. In times of peace and prosperity, dresses featured fitted bodices, full skirts, and natural waistlines. In times of war or economic depression, women wore extreme styles, with very high or very low waistlines, and skirts that were either short or narrow or both. Changes of style often took place during periods of stress. Kroeber concluded that, "since the periods of dress-pattern instability were also periods of marked socio-political instability and churning, there is presumably a connection" [1948, p. 334].

In "What Goes Up, May Stay Up," Marvin Harris [1973] has reexamined the study by Kroeber and Richardson and updated it. He believes that the basic patterns they ascertained had begun to break up in 1913. As for dress length, Kroeber and his coauthor had stated, "the upper limit of possibility and probably our less definable limits of decency" had been reached at the knee. Harris concludes, "They were right in one sense: By surging over the knee the basic pattern had oscillated itself right out of existence" [p. 24]. He agrees with *Vogue*'s statement that "we are past being hung up on hemlines," and predicts that Western women "will never again tolerate a fashion that requires them to wear ankle-to-floor length skirts except as entirely optional alternatives to pants or short skirts. The demise of the floor-length skirt is the Occidental equivalent of the end of foot binding in China or of veil wearing in the Middle East" [p. 24].

THE PROJECT

1. Using several Sears, Roebuck catalogs, trace the history of two different classes of items from different major categories, such as men's boots, lighting fixtures, children's toys, women's bathing suits, or communications equipment. If you do not have access to old or reprinted Sears, Roebuck catalogs (which should be available at most libraries), you might consider working with a sample of issues of some long-established magazine such as *Good Housekeeping*, using either articles or advertisements or both. Analyze the changes that have taken place in the various members of your two classes of artifacts over time. Include in your analysis such things as when new traits appear and when traits disappear.

2. An archaeologist should not attempt to make sweeping generalizations on the basis of tracing changes in only a few classes of artifacts. He does, however, as we suggested, depend a great deal on the information provided by *context* in making his interpretations. Using the same catalog or magazine issues you used for the first portion of the project, suggest some of the ways they provide contextual information about changes in the culture that might aid your interpretation of the changes in the classes of artifacts you examined. For example, does your "contextual material" provide clues about technological changes, periods of economic boom or recession, periods of war or peace, changes in orientation to rural or urban life, changes in the nature and use of leisure time, or changes in the nature of social relations? Note that one of the things upon which you might focus for suggestions is the people pictured, including the size of family groups implied, and so on.

SELECTED ANNOTATED BIBLIOGRAPHY

Clark, J.G.D.
    Archaeology and Society: Reconstructing the Prehistoric Past. Harvard University

Press, rev. ed., 1957. First published London: Methuen & Co., 1939. A well-done study, reprinted several times, concentrates on the Old World.

Daniel, Glyn

The Origins and Growth of Archaeology. Harmondsworth, Middlesex, England: Penguin Books, 1967. Just what it claims to be, including many short sketches on archaeologists and their major accomplishments. The emphasis is on European scholars.

Deetz, James

Invitation to Archaeology. American Museum Science Books, The Natural History Press, 1967. One of many good, basic treatments. Unlike those listed above, this book includes considerable New World material. Inexpensive and convenient, a true "pocket book."

Fagan, Brian M.

In the Beginning: Introduction to Archaeology. Little, Brown, 1972. One of the newest of many introductory treatments, it provides liberally illustrated general coverage.

Gorenstein, Shirley

Introduction to Archaeology. Basic Books, 1965. An especially lucid and pleasantly written book, which carefully introduces each stage of archaeological investigation and, at the same time, gives the reader some sense of the challenge and excitement inherent in much archaeological exploration.

Harris, Marvin

"What Goes Up, May Stay Up." *Natural History,* 1973, LXXII(1):18–25. A new look at an old topic, the changes in women's fashions.

Heizer, Robert F.

The Archaeologist at Work. Harper & Row, 1959. A multifaceted collection of articles by researchers at work in all the various aspects of archaeology.

Heizer, Robert F., and John Graham

A Guide to Field Methods in Archaeology. The National Press, rev. ed., 1967. A thorough guide, well written and illustrated.

Kroeber, Alfred L.

Anthropology. Harcourt, Brace, rev. ed., 1948. Despite its age, an excellent basic text. Mentioned here for its material on culture history and research on women's fashions.

Kroeber, Alfred L., and Jane Richardson

"Three Centuries of Women's Dress Fashions." *Anthropological Records,* 1940, 5–(2):i–iv, 111–153. A classic article on cultural change and women's fashions.

Mayer-Oakes, William J.

Prehistory of the Upper Ohio Valley. Carnegie Museum, 1955. A study of discoveries in a United States valley, noteworthy here as the source of the interesting chart illustrating the use of the seriation method on lighting devices.

Woodall, J. Ned

An Introduction to Modern Archaeology. Schenkman, 1972. A concise, readable, and reasonable summary of some modern approaches to archaeology.

PROJECT NINE
ANALYZING FOLKLORE CONTENT

INTRODUCTION

The philosophy of "art for art's sake" is rarely found among the non-Western people traditionally studied by anthropologists. In such societies, art is often part of economic, political, and religious activities. Indeed, " . . . the artist's work often represents symbolically the essence of the interrelationship between these basic aspects of culture" [Hammond 1971, p. 195]. Artistic expression is seldom restricted to a separate artist class. Verbal as well as graphic art is usually functional, in addition to being decorative or entertaining. For these reasons, anthropologists speak of "folklore" or "folk art," which is, basically, the lore, or the expressed learning, of the "folk," the people.

There are many forms of aesthetic expression that may be studied in terms of their symbolic role in integrating cultural behavior. In the graphic and plastic arts, there are painting, sculpture, and carving. There is instrumental and vocal music and the dance. Tattooing, personal adornment, and head-shrinking may also be considered folk arts in some cultures. But the aspect of folklore that has received by far the most attention from anthropologists has been the oral traditions of society. There are various categories of oral expression that have received particular emphasis.

Myths are generally defined as "traditionally based, dramatic narratives on themes that emphasize the nature of man's relationship to nature and to the supernatural" [Hammond, p. 318]. Most students will be familiar with the myths of ancient

Greece and Rome, which explained the origins of the world, the nature of the gods, and the foundations of the moral system of the world of men. We have come to use the word "myth" as a synonym for any story that is untrue, made-up, or fanciful in some way. Yet, in the anthropological context, the stories of the Bible, or of any living religion, are myths in exactly the same way as are the stories of the no-longer active religions of the ancients. The word "myth" should not be understood as a term of disparagement. Myths can refer to *any* stories that seek to explain why things got to be as they are, regardless of whether or not they are true, and regardless of whether or not they are part of the structure of a living religious system.

On another level, we may also describe certain nonreligious tales as mythic because they explain man's relationship to the impersonal forces around him. A good example is the so-called mythic "Western," which draws on the concept of the frontier as being the breeding ground of a specific type of American personality. The mythic Western hero is the rugged individualist, with his natural sense of justice, honor, and the dignity of labor. Unemotional, the Western hero is forever a stranger riding off into the sunset and on to a new town. It is not important whether such people really existed. They are mythic because they are used, in numerous books, movies, and television tales, as symbols of the relationship between the rugged but bountiful land of the West and the pioneer Americans who tamed the wilderness. In anthropological terms, such a figure is known as a *culture hero* — a character credited with conferring upon mankind special artifacts or institutions, or who has expressed the highest goals of a particular culture.

Legends, in contrast to myths, which often seek to explain *why* things are as they are, thereby providing a traditional moral sanction for action, tend to be more concerned with *how* things got to be as they are. They are more often stories that are told purely for entertainment. They generally lack a supernatural basis, and are seldom as closely identified with the central belief system of a religion or ideology as are myths. Legends may be strictly local in nature, such as stories explaining how a particular deserted house in a certain town is "haunted" by the ghost of a tragic former inhabitant, or they may be well-known nationally, as are the stories of Paul Bunyan, John Henry, and Johnny Appleseed.

The subject of a legend, like the subject of a myth, need not have been a real person, although the American tradition seems particularly rich in legends concerning people whose existence is proven fact, such as Davy Crockett, George Washington, and Abraham Lincoln. In such cases, it becomes difficult to separate out the legendary from the historical aspects of the people: Did Davy Crockett really kill a bear when he was only three? Did George Washington really chop down the cherry tree? Did Abraham Lincoln really walk twenty miles in the snow to return two cents to a grocery customer? Legends are recounted in much the same way as are fairy tales, although they lack the element of the supernatural common to the latter. The purpose of these often amusing or exciting narrative forms is largely instructional. They are entertaining little sermons on various values that the culture holds dear: courage in the face of impersonal power (John Henry), altruism (Johnny Appleseed), the pioneering spirit (Paul Bunyan), honesty (Washington, Lincoln). Not only are they used to teach children these values, they are expressions of the adults' belief in the worth of these attributes.

It is interesting to note that some legends, which appear in various places, reveal subtle shifts in both plot and structure in order to conform to local norms and patterns. For example, the familiar story of Jack and the Beanstalk is found in both England and the United States. The English version emphasizes giving and getting in a balanced, harmonious relationship. It focuses on the theme of a boy doing something noble to help a mother whom he has earlier made to suffer. But in the American version the dominant image, that of the sprouting beanstalk, is also the dominant theme, the theme of individual aspiration. The American story is very much concerned with showing off, and exhibiting elements of male prowess (hunting, fighting), according to Martha Wolfenstein [1965], the scholar who compared the tales. Thus the same story, told in different cultures, will reveal something about the way people in these cultures think about things.

Proverbs may be thought of as shorthand versions of legends that in a sentence or two of witty or otherwise memorable expression present an example of "ethically approved behavior taken from the past or from other places" [Hammond 1971, p. 319]. Proverbs may thus be used as moral guides, for instruction in approved values, and also for indirect social comment or criticism where more open expression would be inappropriate and/or dangerous.

Riddles, in most cultures, are used for entertainment purposes. In our society, they are considered a somewhat childish form of amusement; elsewhere they are used by adults to exercise their wit and their linguistic skill. Moreover,

Their analysis can be useful to the anthropologist interested in acquiring insight into the characteristic patterning of a particular people's mental processes, the symbols that dominate their thought, the manner in which they categorize aspects of reality, and the patterned ways in which they perceive relationships [Hammond, p. 321].

Miscellaneous forms such as verbal abuse, games, nicknaming, toasts, and gossip, or graffiti may also be said to be part of the folklore tradition. The student is directed to Maria Leach [1949–50] for other definitions and explanations of forms studied by the folklorists.

USES OF FOLKLORE ANALYSIS

For the anthropologist, art must be understood as a process whereby certain people do certain things at certain times. As a result, the artistic product is best understood in its cultural and social contexts. Consider, for example, limitations in technology that reduce the available methods of expression; cultural beliefs in what is valuable that direct the activities of the artists toward certain types of expression; limitations in resources that restrict the materials that can be used, and so on.

The artistic product, therefore, is the result of a process both of interpersonal relationships and of relationships between people and their environment. But the product itself may be of great use in an anthropological study, particularly when it is not possible to do a detailed ethnographic analysis of the culture as a whole. One of the first applications of this aspect of folklore analysis was initiated in the World War II period when it became necessary to understand the cultures of the people with whom we were at war, or with whom we were allied but could not visit due to wartime restrictions on travel. Since the war itself made first-hand fieldwork difficult or impossible in many areas, a group of anthropologists determined to study "culture at a distance" and, to this end, analyzed folklore and other manifestations of "popular culture" (magazines, films, books) in order to glean information about the Japanese, German, Russian, and many other cultures. In order to understand the rationale behind this approach, it is necessary to understand that the folk art product is not a passive entity, but rather a medium for learning and transmitting cultural information. If a legend, for example, passes on the knowledge of a cultural value from one member of a society to another, then the analysis of that legend by an anthropologist will enable him to learn which values are being upheld in that society, even if he is not able to verify this conclusion with his own first-hand observations.

Like any product of expressive behavior, folk art may usefully be analyzed on two levels: in terms of its forms, and in terms of its content. Perhaps the most detailed formal analysis of any folk art has been done by Alan Lomax, who developed an elaborate typology of song structures, rhythmical patterns, rhyme schemes, and so on, and correlated these with specific types of social structure. In recent years, there has been an increasing concern with distributional studies of folklore types, in which the elements of the folklore product (particularly characters, types of openings and resolutions, sequences of events) are mapped to show how they have spread, and to determine which types of societies tend to be associated with which types of structure and/or plot motif.

Despite the importance of these formal studies, and the interest that they have generated, it has been the analysis of the content of folklore that has occupied most students of the field to date. The content of anything can be either manifest (obvious, explicit) or latent (hidden, implicit). The artist who creates a particular work of art may have a specific purpose in mind when he is forming his product, which will be the manifest content of his work. But, since he is a member of a cultural tradition, the values, attitudes, and beliefs most commonly held by members of that culture will naturally, and without deliberate attempt, find their way into his work. Moreover, the artist is an individual with his own internalized set of attitudes, beliefs, and personal problems. As a result, the latent content of the work provides a text for the analyst, and he may be able to see those aspects of the culture that are so taken for granted that they turn up even when the artist is making no particular effort to include them.

These points may be illustrated with reference to one particular folk art form: the Trinidad calypso. In the form familiar in the United States and Europe, calypso tends to be associated with a type of ditty with doggerel lyrics sung in a "quaint" island accent to the accompaniment of a gently insistent, danceable beat. But, according to the Trinidadian novelist V.S. Naipaul:

> It is only in the calypso that the Trinidadian touches reality. The calypso is a purely local form. No song composed outside Trinidad

is a calypso. The calypso deals with local incidents, local attitudes, and it does so in a local language. . . . Wit and verbal conceits are fundamental; without them no song, however good the music, however well sung, can be judged a calypso [1962, pp. 75–76].

According to the Trinidadian drama expert Errol Hill, calypso is a form of the "minstrel art"; and he has made a detailed study of the history of the calypso as an independent art form. It is, therefore, appropriate to analyze the calypso to help understand the culture of the Trinidadians who produce it.

Calypso is most closely associated with Carnival, the riotous public theater that is the focus of Trinidad's social life. Each year, just after Christmas, the several dozen professional calypsonians release a set of new calypsoes, songs of personal and social commentary, which are then sung all over the island over the next two and one-half months until Carnival (which occurs on the two days preceding Ash Wednesday, which ushers in the penitential season of Lent). The calypsonian who is judged to have produced the best set of calypsoes for the season will be crowned Calypso King. The individual song that is judged the best and most popular will be named the "Road March," and will be played by the majority of steel bands parading the streets during Carnival. Thus the calypso is not merely any old song; the composition, performance, and judging of calypsoes is a major activity in the life of the people of the island.

Although Trinidad is a nation with a free press and a fairly vigorous radio and television communications network, political and social commentary really come alive only in the singing of calypso. The government, public figures, events, and trends are all fair game for the calypsonian. In the 1971 season, for example, the major topic of conversation was the recent, abortive army mutiny, which was being referred to as the "April Revolution." This event was followed by a strict curfew, the round-up of members of the political opposition, and a sensational military trial. These exciting and important political events were discussed heatedly during the year, and they furnished the subjects for the bulk of the calypsoes for that season.

Lord Kitchener, one of the greatest living calypsonians, entitled his collection of songs for the 1971 season "Curfew Time," and so one might have said that the manifest content of his calypsoes was the new political climate. However, by analyzing some of the songs individually, it is possible to see the latent content, which is very informative, in some ways, about Trinidad society. The calypso "Curfew Time," for example, is not merely a criticism of government policy. It is also a series of amusing double-entendres that leave no doubt in the listeners' minds that Kitch used the order to stay home after dark for purposes other than discussing politics. One of the great traditional themes of calypso, reflecting a preoccupation of Trinidad life, is that of the sexual tug of war between men, who are eager to skip from conquest to conquest, and women, whom the men portray as inevitably surrendering to the superior male magnetism. This statement of an essential value thus comes into a calypso that has a conscious purpose which is quite different. The calypso "PP 99" is manifestly a comment on increasing government interference with private rights, in the form of meter maids who check on the revered island custom of illegal parking. But the resolution of the song suggests that Kitch believes that, if all else fails, he will thwart the meter maids by asserting his masculine sexual dominance over them. "Let Them Crow" is, overtly, a statement in which Kitchener dares the government to cancel Carnival (an action that had been threatened because of fears of renewed outbreaks of violence in the wake of the "revolution"). Covertly, it is a statement of the fundamental Trinidadian belief that no "authority" can push a man around. "I go do what I damn please" is the motto.

Thus, from the analysis of the content of these calypsoes, it is possible to discern not only the manifest concern with the overriding political issues of the day, but also a continuing expression of certain values regarding the expected norms of sociosexual behavior.

In summary, we may say that folklore serves several social functions. The analysis of folklore by the anthropologist can tell us something about the social character of the people who create and use it.

> In addition to the obvious function of entertainment and amusement, folklore serves to sanction the established beliefs, attitudes and institutions, both sacred and secular, and it plays a vital role in education in nonliterate societies. . . . But, in addition to its role in transmitting culture from one generation to another, and to providing ready rationalizations when beliefs and attitudes are called into question, folklore is used in some societies to apply social pressure to those who would deviate from accepted norms . . . beneath a good deal of humor lies a deeper meaning, and . . . folklore serves as a psychological escape from many repressions, not only sexual, which society imposes upon the individual [Bascom 1971, p. 474].

THE PROJECT

Although anthropological studies of folklore have tended to concentrate on the technologically primitive, small-scale societies that are the traditional foci of ethnographic work, it is both possible and desirable to study the folk output of societies such as ours. This task, however, is complicated by the heterogeneity of cultural traditions within American society and by a multilayered creative process which, according to Tristram Coffin and Hennig Cohen [1966], results in a threefold division of folklore products:

- the literary tradition
- the popular tradition
- the oral, or folk, tradition

Since the United States is, generally speaking, a literate society, a large part of our common folk traditions, particularly in the verbal arts, is bound up in material that we have assimilated through the formal education process. Legends such as those of Moby Dick, the celebrated Jumping Frog, Tom and Huck, or the courtship of Miles Standish have all entered our folk consciousness through some recognized literary source. Even those who have never read Longfellow's poem, for example, will know the line, "speak for yourself, John" and will be able to tell the story of which it is a part.

At the other extreme are the oral traditions, which are made up of all the materials that people "who can't, don't, or won't write pass on from generation to generation by word of mouth" [Coffin & Cohen 1966, p. xiii]. Because of the overwhelming influence of literate educational facilities in our culture, our purely oral folk tradition is rapidly dwindling, but it still exists in the form of a number of minor arts, such as proverbs and games. More fully articulated folk narratives (tales, legends, and so on) may still be found relatively intact among the many ethnic, religious, or occupational subcultures in the United States.

The vast middle ground, however, seems to support the bulk of contemporary American folklore. This popular tradition goes back at least as far as the ballads of Stephen Foster, with their self-conscious evocation of the plantation folk styles. To quote Coffin and Cohen:

> The songs of Stephen Foster, George Gershwin, and Bob Dylan which deliberately imitate folk music because it is profitable to do so; the calculated promotion of fictional figures like Pecos Bill and Paul

Bunyan in order to provide the local color that attracts tourists; the transformation by script writers of Billy the Kid and Davy Crockett into television heroes to sell cereal; and even the more or less innocent fabrications of children's stories such as that of George Washington and the cherry tree, designed to teach reading and moral behavior—fall within the popular tradition [Coffin & Cohen 1966, p. xiv].

Although many of these products are consciously created by particular artists or entertainers and are not created by "the folk," they are often vigorous parts of the living folk tradition. For example, Woody Guthrie's depression-era songs about the Dust Bowl and the labor unions are now treated as genuine folk expressions that are much more revealing of "folk" attitudes in a now-distant period than any number of objective history books. More recently, Dylan's "Blowin' in the Wind" has achieved such general acceptance as a popular anthem that its authorship is immaterial—it is a song that supplies a felt need, and has been adopted as a popular statement, just as if it were actually a spontaneously un-self-conscious "folk song."

The folklore analysis project will have two main aspects: the collection of a sample of folkloristic material, and the analysis of its content along the lines suggested above.

Procedure

I. Select one example representative of any one of the three main types of American folklore, as described by Coffin and Cohen. Some suggestions:

A. Literary Tradition (broadly interpreted)
   1. Western novels by Zane Grey.
   2. Epitaphs from old tombstones.
   3. An anthology of *Peanuts* cartoons.
   4. A series of episodes from any popular TV series that features a continuing set of characters.
   5. The student's own collection of graffiti inscriptions.

B. Popular Tradition
   1. The work of a contemporary song composer, either one who is active in the student's local area, and to whom the student has access, or a well-known recording artist.
   2. The student may wish to concentrate on one extended narrative song by a contemporary composer. Note that analyses

of songs such as "American Pie" appear in many places, including dust jackets, and are well known. Please choose something to which you can give a fresh approach without "contamination" from analyses by others.

  C. Oral Tradition
     1. Narratives, legends, tales told by members of special ethnic or occupational subgroups.
     2. Children's playground games.
     3. Proverbs of an ethnic group.
     4. The "real" folk songs.
     5. Jokes and riddles.

The student is also directed to Clarke [1963] for a more detailed survey of possible folklore topics that might readily be collected by the nonprofessional.

  II. Make sure that you have full texts to work with. If you are dealing with songs, the lyrics should be available to people reading your report; these may be in the form of printed sheet music, or as a transcript of a recorded performance. When collecting nonwritten material, such as proverbs, it is best to tape the informant who is reciting. For nonverbal activities, a series of photos would be helpful for a reader trying to follow your analysis.

 III. Although the student will want to say a few words regarding the structure of a piece of folklore with which he is dealing, the report should be geared toward an investigation of the *content* of the pieces under analysis.

 IV. For the piece of folklore which you have chosen, write a brief summary considering as many of the following questions as may be relevant to it.

  A. What is the piece of folklore which you have chosen? Describe it. Describe the context in which it is typically found. Discuss how you collected it. Who else beside the performer was present? Under what circumstances? What was the atmosphere like (i.e., somber or happy, reverent or lighthearted)?

  B. What is the source of the material in both time and place? For example, a collection of Yiddish proverbs might be collected in New York City, 1973, but derived from Eastern Europe, circa 1750.

1. **The** question of provenience (the source of the material in time and place) also includes the question of influences: what (if any) sources outside the community in which this piece is performed influenced the adoption of this folk form? What (if any) other arts in other communities have been affected by this folk form?

C. Is the piece of folklore typically the work of one individual artist or group of artists? If so, how is he (or are they) identified? If not, who also performs it? In what ways have the form and content changed by passing through other hands? For example, although a popular song like "Blowin' in the Wind" has a set of copyrighted lyrics, do other people who typically sing the song tend to change certain of the lyrics? If so, which ones? How? Why?

D. What are the recurring motifs in this piece of folklore?
   1. Verbal phrases.
   2. Physical activities by both the performer and his audience that are associated with the piece.
   3. The style that is appropriate to the performance of the piece.
   4. Is it mythic or legendary in any way? How? To what social goals (if any) is the myth or legend directed?

E. What are the recurring themes of the piece? Which values, attitudes, or behavior norms do they uphold? How? Is the piece used to teach these attitudes to children or other individuals coming into this society? Which of these themes is manifest in the work? Which are latent? How can you account for this?

F. Are the expressed values, attitudes, or behavior norms typical of the group as a whole (in which case the artist is merely reflecting such norms), or is the artist trying to impose his values on his society?

The student is directed to Crowley [1966] for an example of this type of analysis as applied to an extended set of folk narratives.

After completion of this analysis, three students who selected pieces representing the three different aspects of contemporary American folk art might want to make a joint presentation to discuss the differences in the three types, as well as the similarities, if any.

Some further suggestions:

I. When gathering data from a live informant:
   A. Be sure you have made observations and/or recordings on at

least two occasions, if at all possible, in order to verify that lyrics, actions, styles, and so on, are really part of the work and not just temporary accidents.

B. As a general rule, older people are much better sources of information about folklore than young people, even when it comes to typical children's lore, such as fairy tales or games. But do not overlook the fact that children or adolescents have a folklore of their own, even if it is not rooted in many generations of tradition. Such behavior will be less obvious to the casual observer, but if the student is in prolonged contact with a group of young people (perhaps from being involved with them for another project in this book), he may be able to get a clearer picture of their own particular folklore. One possible field of analysis in this context might be slang vocabulary, which has a very fast turnover rate.

II. When reporting the data:

A. Be sure that your sources of information are clearly indicated. Provide transcriptions of taped interviews, references to published sources, and photo series of nonverbal behavior wherever relevant, and wherever feasible.

III. When analyzing the data:

A. Remember that when dealing with the popular and oral traditions, it will not always be possible to work with an extended corpus or body of materials. In the literary tradition, it is possible to say definitely that a certain collection of stories about the Old West represents the unified vision of a known author, for example, Zane Grey. However, when working with the more diffuse forms, such as a song by a composer who has done nothing else with which one is familiar, or with scattered productions like graffiti, it is unwise to strain after consistency or unifying themes. Nevertheless, because even these arts are, to one degree or another, socially conditioned, they will reveal certain themes and patterns that they have in common with other productions of the same culture. Even a nonunified collection of materials (political slogans painted on walls during an uprising) can be analyzed to show certain dominant social themes.

SELECTED ANNOTATED BIBLIOGRAPHY

Abrahams, Roger
"The Toast: A Neglected Form of Folk Narrative." In Horace P. Beck, ed., *Folklore in Action.* The American Folklore Society, 1962. A leading contemporary folklorist discusses a minor but intriguing example of American folklore.

Barnouw, Victor
Culture and Personality. Dorsey, 1963. Includes a good chapter on art and folklore as expressions of the personality of the individual artist, as well as mirrors of dominant social and cultural values.

Bascom, William R.
"Folklore and Anthropology." In Lowell D. Holmes, ed., *Readings in General Anthropology.* Ronald, 1971. A clear and concise abridgement of a longer article spelling out the uses of folklore analysis for the anthropologist.

Clarke, Kenneth W., and Mary W. Clarke
Introducing Folklore. Holt, Rinehart and Winston, 1963. A good, basic manual that describes various folklore types, and provides some interesting suggestions for the collection and analysis of such material.

Coffin, Tristram P., and Hennig Cohen
Folklore in America. Anchor Books, 1966. An excellent, heterogeneous collection of folk productions in the U.S.

Creighton, Helen
"Cape Breton Nicknames and Tales." In Horace P. Beck, ed., *Folklore in Action.* The American Folklore Society, 1962. A lively discussion of a minor but interesting form of folklore as found in a distinctive culture.

Crowley, Daniel J.
I Could Talk Old-Story Good: Creativity in Bahamian Folklore. University of California Press, 1966. A sociocultural analysis of folk products; entertaining reading in addition to being a good model for the student's own analysis.

Dundes, Alan
"Structural Typologies in North American Indian Folktales." In Alan Dundes, ed., *The Study of Folklore.* Prentice-Hall, 1965. An example of formal and distributional analysis in folklore.

Edmonson, Munro
Lore: An Introduction to the Science of Folklore and Literature. Holt, Rinehart and Winston, 1971. A very highly regarded recent survey of the field of anthropology and folklore; tackles theoretical, as well as methodological, issues in the study of traditional literature.

Hammond, Peter B.
An Introduction to Cultural and Social Anthropology. Macmillan, 1971. Some good, basic information on the use of folklore analysis in anthropology.

Hill, Errol
The Trinidad Carnival. University of Texas Press, 1972. A scholarly and beautifully illustrated analysis of a folk art.

Jansen, Hugh
"Riddles: The 'Do-it-yourself Oracles'." In Tristram Coffin, ed., *Our Living Traditions: An Introduction to American Folklore.* Basic Books, 1968. A concise

discussion of a broad, anthropologically useful form of folk literature.

Krappe, Alexander H.

The Science of Folklore. Norton, 1964. An erudite guide to research in the field of folklore analysis.

Leach, Maria, ed.

Standard Dictionary of Folklore, Mythology and Legend. 2 vols., Funk and Wagnalls, 1949–50. A standard reference work in the field.

Lomax, Alan J.

Folk Song Style and Culture. American Association for the Advancement of Science, 1968. An exhaustive compendium of research in the field of song structure as related to social structure.

Mead, Margaret, and Rhoda Metraux

The Study of Culture at a Distance. University of Chicago Press, 1953. The classic exposition of the uses of the popular arts in studying other cultures.

Mockridge, Norton

The Scrawl of the Wild. World, 1958. A witty description of graffiti, past and present.

Naipaul, V.S.

The Middle Passage. London: A. Deutsch, 1962. Naipaul's comments on calypso and Carnival are perhaps overly chauvinistic, but they are good examples of the influence of folklore on social values. Naipaul's outlook also demonstrates how one West Indian was "socialized" into political consciousness via a folk art, the calypso.

Ross, G.

"Revolution on the Walls: Paris." *Nation,* 1968, 207:84–85. Slogans painted on the walls during the student uprising are a clue to the values of the protesters.

Schapiro, Meyer

"Style." In A.L. Kroeber, ed., *Anthropology Today.* University of Chicago Press, 1952. A classic exposition of the theory of content analysis.

Sutton-Smith, Brian

"The Folk Games of Children." In Tristram Coffin, ed., *Our Living Traditions: An Introduction to American Folklore.* Basic Books, 1968. A summary of research into a form of folklore in the non-literary sphere.

Walker, R.J.

"Kilroy Was Here: A History of Scribbling in Ancient and Modern Times." *Hobbies,* 1968, 73:98N–98O. A lively account of the study of wall inscriptions, now known as the science of graffiti analysis.

Wallace, A.F.C.

"A Possible Technique for Recognizing Psychological Characteristics of the Ancient Maya from an Analysis of Their Art." *American Imago,* 1950, 7:239–258. A theoretical analysis of Mayan artistic products that aims at making inferences about the culture in which they were produced and about the personalities of the individuals who produced them.

Wolfenstein, Martha

"Jack and the Beanstalk: An American Version." In Alan Dundes, ed., *The Study of Folklore.* Prentice-Hall, 1965. This article originally appeared in a volume on childhood in contemporary societies edited by **Mead and Wolfen-stein**, and it has been anthologized in several editions. Since this chapter deals with folklore, it is probably most convenient to read the article in the context of other folklore articles.

PROJECT TEN

DOING ETHNOSEMANTIC RESEARCH

INTRODUCTION

The two main activities of anthropological research are the collection and interpretation of information. Ideally, ethnography, the process of collecting material in the field, should be descriptive, and based on the objective collection of observed or recorded events. A random catalog of descriptions would not constitute good anthropology, however, since all the facts and figures need to be classified, organized, and interpreted in such a way as to give the reader a coherent view of what the culture in question is all about.

There has been some debate among anthropologists as to the proper means of classifying cultural data. All anthropologists would agree that the sources of the most basic data are one's native informants. But many anthropologists feel that any conceptual framework that gives structure to these data must arise out of the theories of the anthropologist himself. This is because he has a cross-cultural perspective as a result of his studies and, thus, can fit the data of one culture into a broader, more nearly global framework. Since the study of *phonetics* utilizes a set of internationally standardized symbols (the International Phonetic Alphabet) for recording all the many languages of the world, the type of ethnography that utilizes a similarly global framework for analyzing cultural data has been named the *etic* strategy for fieldwork.

On the other hand, there are other anthropologists who believe that for us to impose our own categories for classification is ethnocentric. These researchers feel that any organization of the data should be based on the "homemade models," or inside views, of the native informants themselves. In linguistics, the study of the contrastive distributions of sounds that can be used to signal changes in meaning to native speakers of the language is known as *phonemics*. By analogy, the "homemade model" treatment of other cultural data is known as the *emic* approach. Unfortunately, *emic* and *etic* have become slogans or catchwords in anthropology, rather than clear-cut concepts. The student should be aware that they are used differently by different theorists, although in one way or another they all refer to this linguistic model, and are ultimately based on the assumption that, since language is the most basic cultural institution, the models by which it is studied can also guide the study of other human institutions.

It may be noted that language is, in many ways, a distinctively human attribute. All animals can communicate with each other, and many of the higher primates have very elaborate call systems. But only man has the capacity to use language, in the sense of a set of arbitrary sound symbols that can be used to deal in abstractions, combined to create new symbols, and strung together according to certain rules (grammar) to produce lengthy, meaningful utterances. Although chimpanzees in experimental situations have been taught to use certain aspects of language that were once thought to be exclusively human, there is as yet no evidence that they do so in nature. We speak of the symbols of language as being arbitrary because their meaning is bestowed upon them by those who use them in communication. Thus while a chimp may, under controlled conditions, be capable of learning some of the symbols of a given human language, the fact that he cannot himself create symbols indicates that his own communication system (even if we were willing to call it a language) is somehow different from ours.

The use of abstract concepts possibly accompanied the invention of the first human tools, and a case may be made for the hypothesis that the refinements of tool manufacture and the elaboration of culture that went with such refinements stimulated a growth in language usage. Similarly, the use of increasingly complex language made possible the invention and utilization of more complex elements of culture.

Language is the aspect of culture that comes closest to being "predictable" in the rigorously scientific sense. Every language has certain logical rules (for pronunciation, for word formation, and for grammar) whose structure can be charted and classified.

For these reasons, language is often taken as a model by which other cultural activities may be studied.

In other projects in this book, you will be able to practice a number of standard *etic* methods for the collection of data, such as the standardized survey in Project 11. In this project, however, you will be able to try one typical sort of *emic* strategy, which is now known as *ethnosemantics* (but, when it was first introduced, was called "the new ethnography").

Before proceeding to the project, it will be necessary to understand something of the background of *emic* research. This strategy is most characteristically used by anthropologists who also have a strong interest in the specialized subfield of anthropological linguistics. However, the method can be used rather conveniently by fieldworkers with other subfield interests, as long as they pay heed to a few basic concepts.

One major aspect of ethnosemantics is the proposition that different cultures, like different languages, have their own specific rules and logical structures. (According to many linguists, these differences are merely on the surface, for at the "deepest" levels, all human languages share important structures. This consideration, however, is not immediately relevant to the performance of this project.) All languages meet the same basic need of communication, but this need is answered in hundreds of different ways by the various languages of the world. In the same way, any culture is, in part, an adaptive mechanism that helps people cope with the physical environments in which they find themselves; yet if "survival" is the goal of all cultures, there are many different ways cultures go about the task. Since languages must have rules and patterns in order to be used efficiently as communicative "codes," it is possible for a native speaker of one language to learn to recognize the regularities of another and, hence, learn to use another language. Similarly, if different cultures were lacking in logical rules, then there would be no science of anthropology, since it would be impossible for a person born in one culture ever to learn the culture of another group. Therefore, just as the linguist studies the rules by which the structure of a language is built up, so the ethnographer can study the units of culture and discover the ways in which these units fit together to form a coherent, more or less consistent, scheme that makes sense to the people living within that culture.

One small linguistic example should suffice for illustration. In English, when we say the word "kill" and contrast it to "gill," any native informant would say that the two utterances have quite different meanings. Since everything about these utterances is alike except for the initial consonant sounds, we can assume that the difference between the two signals a change in meaning. "K" and "g" are therefore distinct sounds in English. We say that they are different *phonemes*. Now say the word "ski" and then the word "key." You can hear, if you listen carefully, that two distinct "k" sounds are being produced. The "k" in "k^{h}ey" has a small but noticeable added puff of breath (aspiration) that the "k" in "ski" lacks. Nevertheless, in English we do not necessarily perceive any contrast between the two sounds. In fact, if we put the aspirated "k" in the other place and say "sk^{h}i" it would still mean the same thing to any other native speaker of English, although, admittedly, it might sound peculiar. Therefore, the two separate "k" sounds are considered to be part of one phoneme, since they do not contrast with each other in the same meaningful way that "k" and "g" do. In Hindi, on the other hand, there is an important difference between consonants that are aspirated and those that are not, and this difference would signal a change in meaning in any word in which the consonants in question appeared. Thus, in Hindi the word "k^{h}il" ("grain") is obviously different from the word "kil" ("nail") so that the variation between "k^h" and "k" is meaningful. They are thus separate phonemes in Hindi. Since this is a regular practice, a native speaker of English must remember to make such distinctions when he learns Hindi, although he ordinarily would not think of it while speaking English. [See Gleason 1961, Chapter 15.]

The same pattern holds true for other aspects of culture. One well-known example is that of color terms. In English, we are used to the familiar ROYGBIV breakdown of the spectrum (red, orange, yellow, green, blue, indigo, violet). But there is nothing in the nature of the continuous gradation of the spectrum that enforces this categorization — it is a purely conventionalized division, devised and employed by speakers of English. Each language has its own conventional terminology. Compared to English, Shona (a language of Rhodesia) and Bassa (a language of Liberia) do it in the following ways:

ENGLISH	purple	blue	green	yellow	orange	red
SHONA	cips^{w}uka	citema	cicena		cips^{w}uka	
BASSA		hui		ziza		

[Gleason 1961:4]

More recent investigations have suggested that certain aspects of color terminology (the black/white contrast, for example) are universal, so that systems of classification may basically be elaborate variants on fundamental human themes [Berlin & Kay 1969]. If so, it becomes even more important to study such manifestations of cultural variation in order to be able to sort out meaningful variations from mere random variations on the same universal pattern. Each culture will establish its own rules for setting the boundaries around categories; thus what one "knows" (the process of cognition) is influenced by what one is taught to filter out of one's overall perceptual field.

In part, these culturally defined boundaries are set by the criterion of relative importance. For example, it is a familiar story that Eskimos have no word for snow, but that they have many different words for different kinds of snow. Though someone from a temperate climate would see only one thing, "snow," and it would scarcely matter to him if it were icy, wet, hard-packed, loose, drifting, or anything else, to the Eskimo, whose survival depends on his being able to be very precise about such environmental conditions, such apparently trivial distinctions take on great significance. Eskimos therefore "see" and designate differences that someone from another culture would not.

On the other hand, if an Eskimo who had lived his entire life in the Arctic paid a visit to a large city in Canada or the United States, he would be impressed by the many vehicles he saw in the streets, all of which were metallic, had four wheels, and were driven by some unseen force within the body of the object. He would, if he were of a curious temperament, begin asking people, "What is that thing?" He would most likely be told, "It's a car." If he got the same answer every time he pointed to a vehicle, he might well come to the conclusion that "These things are all cars, and all cars are pretty much alike." But we are well aware of the fact that all cars are not alike. Even those among us who are least car-conscious make all sorts of critical distinctions among them, having to do with size, shape, type of engine, type of accessories, country of manufacture, year of manufacture, and so on. We do this because cars have become important in our lives in many ways. We even invest different kinds of cars with emotional, value-laden symbolism. Driving a Mercedes-Benz is emphatically not "just the same" as driving a Volkswagen to us, although both are made in Germany.

What our hypothetical Eskimo failed to do was to dig deeper into the ways in which Canadians or Americans distinguish among their vehicles. He had asked too broad a question; and, although he had established the important criteria by which the outer limits of the category "car" were bounded, he had learned nothing about the equally important criteria that distinguish different cars within the category. He would, therefore, be at a loss if he ever had to deal with any particular car. He might not, for example, be able to make the distinction between a taxi and a private car since, to his eyes, they "look alike." This situation would be analogous to one in which a person would be unable to learn a new language if he never learned to understand the contrasts among the phonemes of that language.

The problem, then, is to define the *semantic domain* — the boundaries of the meanings — for certain broadly applied terms. This is done by establishing a paradigm — model — of that aspect of the culture being studied, by asking certain questions, beginning with the most general and proceeding to the most specific. In the case of our Eskimo and the cars, he might first say to an informant, "I've been hearing the word 'car' a lot since I've been here. Tell me, what is a 'car'?" The informant would answer something to the effect that a car is a four-wheeled vehicle powered by some sort of fuel that is burned inside the body of the vehicle. At this point, a basic question might be, "What types of cars are there?" One might also ask, "What are the different things a car has?" or "What are the different things a car does?" Since such questions may help establish the boundaries of categories, they are known as *structural questions*. Questions of a similar type that establish the boundaries of abstract concepts (rather than of material items) would be known as *attribute questions*.

These criteria set the outer bounds of the semantic domain of the term "car." The Eskimo ethnographer would then review with his informant a variety of items, all of which are "cars" but some of which are different from others in the group, on the basis of the informant's own definition of "difference." The Eskimo might first mention that all of the items are painted different colors. "Can the cars be classified as to color?" he might ask. He would probably be told that, although colors may be important when one is choosing a car to buy for one's own use, it is not really a means of classifying cars, since all blue cars in the world do not necessarily share anything of great importance beyond the color. Therefore, color is not a high-level criterion within this domain, although it may be important as the domain is narrowed down very sharply. The Eskimo would then go on to point out various other features that he noticed. He would inquire whether they were significant in classifying cars. "Does the fact that this one has three pedals on the floor while this one has only two mean anything?" he would ask, and learn the important distinction between "standard" and "automatic." Therefore, we now know that we have a second level of significance.

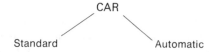

The next step would be to discover what components of a standard transmission car distinguish it from a car with automatic transmission. The ethnographer might then learn that, as far as the driver is concerned, the main difference involves a certain action known as "shifting," or moving a stick in coordination with working the pedals on the standard car, an activity that does not take place in an automatic. In essence, he would learn that in order to make the engine of any car work, its moving parts must be realigned with each other each time the speed of the vehicle changes. This realignment is done within the engine itself in an "automatic" but must be done by the driver manipulating his stick and pedals in a "standard" car. Of course, if the informant were an auto mechanic or car salesman rather than an ordinary driver, he would probably cite other criteria for distinguishing between the two.

However, knowing all of this would not be very helpful to the Eskimo, important as the information is in and of itself. If he again asked what else helped one to tell one car from another, he might learn that there are other distinctions that cut across the standard/automatic dichotomy. For example, he might learn that cars burn gasoline as fuel, and that it is important for people to know how much fuel their cars need to use. Although, as a general rule, standard transmission cars are more economical as to fuel consumption than automatics, high and low consumption of gasoline are subsets of both of the broader categories.

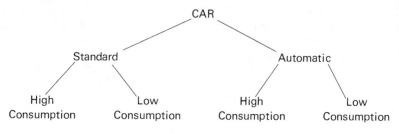

To be sure, the ethnographer would need to get a clear definition from the informant as to what he thinks constitutes "high" versus "low" fuel consumption.

There are, of course, many more than four types of cars, and numerous other criteria besides those already listed. But further questions would elicit all of the standards that the informant feels to be important in categorizing any car he might ever run across. Remember that the paradigm represents the *informant's* view of the world; it may or may not be the same categorization someone else would give. In fact, critics of the ethnosemantic approach, like Robbins Burling, have pointed out that the "logical possibilities" of classifying terms are so numerous that there might be no way to tell which of several possible models is the one that is "psychologically real" [1964, p. 26]. It is for this reason that a specialist or expert should be chosen as the informant, since his view will most closely approach the culturally accepted standard. In our society, the nomenclature of plants, for instance, if elicited from a botanist, would be quite different from that elicited from a Saturday gardener, because their expertise reflects different concerns with plants. In our society, science and the folk tradition are quite separate categories—one might almost say parts of separate cultures—although in most traditional or "primitive" societies, the folk culture *is* the science. Thus, ethnosemanticists working in traditional societies need not fear that their expert's view will not be representative, although those working in our own society must necessarily be more explicit in defining for which segments of the culture their informants are "experts."

When the paradigm is completed, the ethnographer will have a full model of the cognitive "map" of the informant. He will, for example, understand all of the defining dimensions of the domain "car," and he, too, will be able to tell the differences among cars, even though he is not a native of a culture that ordinarily makes such distinctions.

One other means of generating a paradigm is to employ the method of "levels of contrast." For example, if we are interested in working out a classification of different types of animals, and we see a poodle and ask an informant, "Is it a plant?" "Is it a cat?" "Is it a collie?" we are eliciting information about three distinct levels of contrast. In the first case, the answer would be "No, it's an animal"; then, "No, it's a dog"; and finally, "No, it's a poodle." Therefore, we have learned that there are at least three levels of discrimination for classifying this object:

```
ANIMAL – contrasts with – PLANT

DOG – contrasts with – CAT (two different kinds of animal)

POODLE – contrasts with – COLLIE (two different kinds of dog)
```

One must be particularly cautious in dealing with contrast-level types of questions because several words contrast at so many different levels. In English, for example, the term "man," with the somewhat spiritual meaning of "human," can contrast with "animal," although at a more inclusive level "man" is merely one kind of animal. At a more specific level, "man" contrasts with "woman" or "boy" or even one of several terms indicating an "unmanly" man. [See Frake 1961 for a more thorough discussion of these problems.] Remember, though, that even if the same word is used in a variety of meanings, there can be no category established as a semantic domain unless it contrasts with something else.

It is sometimes charged that the method of ethnosemantics is "too logical" – that people really never think about making such precise definitions unless they are prodded to do so by the inquisitive ethnographer. This is probably true. It is also likely that few people really care why one thing is, say, a "fruit" and something else is a "vegetable," as the important thing is to eat them, not analyze them. But the point is that even though they may not make such distinctions as precisely or as frequently as the ethnographer might hope, they still maintain the cognitive structure typical of their culture, and everything that they experience is ultimately filtered through the "map" that unconsciously sets out the boundary markers of what they see or experience. Thus, by studying the cognitive structure in this way, one can learn a great deal about how people strive to make some logical sense out of the welter of their perceptions.

Another criticism of the ethnosemantic method concerns its somewhat picayune nature. One may learn a lot about a plant, or a color, or a car by doing this, but is not such information trivial in the general scheme of things? And does it not take so long to elicit the paradigm of one minor aspect of a culture that we could never hope to use this method to study an entire culture? It is true that the ethnosemantic method would be quite tedious if every minute aspect of a culture were followed up in this detailed way. But, despite this methodological drawback, the theory remains sound. If one is convinced of the value of eliciting "home-made models" for understanding a culture, then ethnosemantics is a valid and highly informative way of going about it.

THE PROJECT

Select a semantic domain and create a paradigm for it. The first step is to select an informant with whom to work. Ideally, one might want to work with several informants in order to make sure that the answers one gets are truly representative. But many ethnosemantics specialists have gotten their results by working with only one informant who also happened to be a specialist or expert in whatever domain was being investigated. For example, if one were interested in the category of "plants," a good person to interview might be a gardener. In some instances, a curer (herbalist, shaman, etc.) would also be familiar with many types of plants because he or she would use them in the act of curing. One could elicit information on how to tell one plant from another from this person. Plants might be distinguished on the basis of what they look like, what they are used for, where they grow, and so on.

You may wish to start with a relatively simple domain, one that you feel has only a few critical dimensions. One example might be to draw up a paradigm of the various types of burger concoctions served at one of the popular fast-food stands. If you are then feeling adventurous, or if you have some extra time, you may want to tackle something a bit more complex, such as interviewing a real estate agent about types of houses. You can use the real estate ads in the newspapers for clues as to what may be some of the critical dimensions of the category of "dwellings": size of the rooms, number of rooms, location, special appliances, and so forth, are all used to differentiate one type of house from another. A yachtsman might be interviewed in the same way about types of boats.

If you speak another language, or have access to a bilingual informant, you may also want to try to compare the boundaries of domains cross-linguistically (and, by extension, cross-culturally). This latter approach can be tried as a team effort. One student may interview an American cook in order to generate a paradigm of types of kitchen utensils, while someone else interviews a French, Italian, Indian, or Chinese cook about the utensils used in those cooking traditions. Even languages as closely related as English and French, which might be expected to produce much the same sort of linguistic patterning, will be likely to have quite different boundaries within the domain of cookware, since the role of cookery is quite different in French culture than it is in American. One object of ethnosemantic research is to be able to "see" and deal with "reality" in the way that a native of the culture under study sees and deals with it. Therefore, although these several cooking traditions will each have features that have no precise parallels in the others, certain criteria for establishing the domains will remain constant. For example, each one will have at least one thing used for stirring, as this is a motion required in virtually all styles of preparing food. It is, however, both interesting and important to see that in one tradition the stirring "thing" may be metallic and rounded while in another it will be flat and wooden, and so forth.

The following example demonstrates regional variation in dealing with a category with which all people in our society are familiar: footwear. If you followed up on this model in your own area, you might well get some different responses and, hence, a very different paradigm.

You may begin to interview your informant by asking a very general question, such as "What kinds of shoes do you sell in your store?" It is then important to check whether the answers are all on the same level of contrast. For example, the informant might say, "We sell dress shoes, sneakers, sandals, and deck shoes." But, upon further questioning, you would learn that "dress shoes/sneakers" are not precisely a contrastive pair, because "dress shoes" is a very broad, general category, whereas "sneakers" is a specific case. Therefore, sneakers, sandals, and deck shoes are all examples of a broader category of "leisure shoes," which does form a contrastive pair with "dress shoes." Thus, you can ask your informant to name various examples of dress shoes that would contrast, on their own level, with the examples of leisure shoes.

Next, you might want the informant to help you understand the criteria for distinguishing between dress and leisure shoes (what they look like, materials used in their creation, when and how they are used, etc.). You can do this with the more specific categories as well; thus, you would want to ask how to tell the difference between a "sneaker" (which, in some areas, means only that sort of lace-up canvas shoe with ridged rubber soles and an extra pad of rubber covering the toes on top) and a "tennis shoe" (which can refer to lace-up canvas shoes that have flat rubber soles and no toe pad) within the larger category of "leisure wear." In preparing this project, we asked this question of numerous friends, both students and professional anthropologists, and got almost as many different answers as there were informants. People from certain regions of the United States make no distinction at all between "sneaker" and "tennis shoe," while others from different regions feel that "sneakers" are a variety of "tennis shoe," or vice versa. Others insisted that they were, in fact, distinct types, but specified criteria other than the ones listed above for distinguishing between them. This indicates, perhaps, that the example was not well chosen—it is such an unimportant part of our culture that people are very careless about using the terms. But, in another sense, it is a highly illustrative example in two ways. In the first place, it indicates that something that we take for granted as a known quantity is not nearly as "known" as we think. If people from the same culture (but having been brought up in various regions) can misunderstand each other and not recognize that different people will have different structures of meaning for the same term, then imagine the problem in translating knowledge across a much wider cultural gap. The theory and method of ethnosemantics makes us very much aware of how relative our knowledge can be. In the second place, the example illustrates the contention that the job of the ethnosemantic researcher is to discover the meaningful criteria in his informant's terms, not in his own. The broader question of whether the information thus gained truly represents "everybody" has not yet been satisfactorily answered. The point here, however, is to use the method in order to elicit data, for, without that, the question of representativeness can never be answered at all.

Your report should include a list of the questions you used in establishing your structures, as well as an outline of the completed paradigm itself.

SELECTED ANNOTATED BIBLIOGRAPHY

Basso, Keith H.
  Western Apache Witchcraft. Anthropological Papers of the University of Arizona 15, 1969. An application of the ethnosemantic approach to a broad area of cultural behavior rather than to specific, individual items.
Berlin, B., and P. Kay
  Basic Color Terms: Their Universality and Evolution. University of California Press, 1969. A recent and provocative study in which much-studied terminology is reexamined. The authors feel that it is in this aspect of the comparative study of language that certain structural universals are to be found; and, on the basis of this assumption, they propose a theory of the evolution of color terminology.
Burling, Robbins
  "Cognition and Componential Analysis: God's Truth or Hocus-Pocus?" *American Anthropologist,* 1964, 66:20–28. A critical survey of the theory behind ethnosemantic research.
Conklin, Harold C.
  "Hanunoo Color Categories." *Southwestern Journal of Anthropology,* 1955,

11:**339**–344. One of the most widely cited ethnosemantic studies.

Frake, Charles O.

"Diagnosis of Disease among the Subanun of Mindanao." *American Anthropologist,* 1961, 63:113–132. Another pioneering ethnosemantic study dealing with categories of disease; contains some useful models for the creation of paradigms.

Gleason, H. A.

An Introduction to Descriptive Linguistics. Holt, Rinehart and Winston, rev. ed., 1961. A standard textbook in linguistic analysis that may be of some help to the student interested in learning some more about the linguistic background that is so important to ethnosemantic research. The textbook is accompanied by a workbook of linguistic problems.

Hockett, Charles F.

"Chinese versus English; An Exploration of the Whorfian Theses." In Harry Hoijer, ed., *Language in Culture.* American Anthropological Association, Memoir No. 79, 1954. A brief, readable account of the cognitive differences between two language/culture systems.

Keesing, Roger M.

"Paradigms Lost: The New Ethnography and the New Linguistics." *Southwestern Journal of Anthropology,* 1972, 28:299–332. A critical survey of the status of ethnosemantic research today.

Sapir, Edward

Language. Harcourt, Brace and World, 1921. A standard work by one of the pioneers of anthropological linguistics.

Spradley, James P.

Culture and Cognition: Rules, Maps and Plans. Chandler, 1972. A general survey of the state of "cognitive anthropology" today; it is a much more sympathetic account than either the Burling or the Keesing article.

Spradley, James P., and David W. McCurdy

The Cultural Experience: Ethnography in Complex Society. Science Research Associates, 1972. A concise manual for doing ethnosemantic types of ethnography; also includes a collection of such ethnographies produced by undergraduate students. Students who are particularly interested in following up on ethnosemantic types of studies will find this a useful guide to some of the more refined techniques for establishing paradigms and dealing with other aspects of the general problems touched upon in this chapter.

Tyler, Stephen A., ed.

Cognitive Anthropology. Holt, Rinehart and Winston, 1969. Another sympathetic summary of the field.

Wallace, Anthony F.C., and John Atkins

"The Meaning of Kinship Terms." *American Anthropologist,* 1960, 62:58–80. A widely discussed application of the paradigmatic model to the study of kinship terminology. Kinship is one area of culture that seems to come close to language in being patterned into definite, cognitively defined structures.

PROJECT ELEVEN

USING A STANDARDIZED QUESTIONNAIRE

INTRODUCTION

Although the ethnographer very often creates his own research instruments in the field, it is sometimes useful for him to employ some sort of questionnaire or other survey instrument that has been developed in another field situation and has been standardized for cross-cultural research. Every cultural setting is, of course, unique in some ways. But, since one aim of anthropology is to collect data to support generalizations about human behavior in a wide variety of situations, it should be possible to compare the data of one culture with that of another.

The bulk of an anthropologist's time in the field is devoted to unstructured interviewing and informal observations. As a result, it may be difficult to compare perceptions of one anthropologist working in one culture with those of a colleague working somewhere else. If both, however, are interested in the same general type of problem, such as the relationship between social change and emotional stress, then it would be valuable to be able to translate their respective perceptions into each other's terms. For this reason, it is advisable to make use of one or more cross-culturally standardized tests in order to report on data that might potentially be used by anthropologists working elsewhere, or even in the same area at a later date.

Any standardized behavioral index is the result of one general hypothesis (or limited series of related hypotheses) that can be thought of as asking the question, "If X is present in this community, will we tend to find Y associated with it?" The index or questionnaire is thus a series of questions or measurements designed to test for the presence of both X and Y. Statistical analysis of these results tells the researcher whether or not there is a meaningful correlation between the two in his particular group.

In anthropology, no standardized questionnaire can ever be considered to be the sum total of one's field research. The data yielded by such a technique are always expressed in terms of general trends. These data are, in a sense, the skeleton of one's analysis, in that they supply a framework for suggesting explanations for certain behavior. But the flesh that covers the skeleton, the descriptive material that makes the questionnaire's abstract categories into real human behavior, can best come from the more personalized, unstructured observational and interviewing techniques discussed in earlier projects in this book.

In spite of this limitation on standardized surveys, they are an especially valuable research aid and are becoming increasingly important as the trend in contemporary anthropology moves away from general ethnographies of cultures (there being fewer and fewer "untouched" societies) and toward the investigation of specific problems or limited areas of behavior within a given culture. The anthropology student should, therefore, be acquainted with the process of hypothesis formulation and testing, and with the application of standardized survey techniques.

THE HEALTH OPINION SURVEY

There are numerous standardized indices and measures developed for use by behavioral scientists, although most of these seem to be more relevant to sociology or psychology than to ethnography. However, for the purposes of this project, we will consider one questionnaire that was designed in a specifically anthropological context, and has been used with much success by anthropologists. This instrument is known as the Health Opinion Survey (HOS).

The HOS was first devised by Allister Macmillan and later developed by Alexander Leighton and his associates at Cornell University in the 1950s. Their working hypothesis was that all individuals, in all cultures, exist in a state of striving toward certain culturally approved goals. Some individuals are incapable of attaining these goals because they are personally unable to cope with their environments. Other individuals fail to attain them because their society has become disrupted, or is in the process of rapid change (or "disintegration") and no longer provides the proper channels for reaching traditional goals. In either case, individuals who are not able to manage the stress caused by their blocked striving are the ones most likely to exhibit symptoms of their distress.

The HOS is a set of twenty questions that inquire about common physiological responses that the body makes to what is perceived as stress. All mammals react in much the same way to stress: increased rate of heartbeat, sweating, poor sleep, and similar symptoms; but in humans there is great variety in the definition of what is or is not stressful. As a result, the HOS is designed to measure the extent of "psychophysiological" stress. It does not, of itself, indicate the reasons why the individual *perceives himself* to be under stress. Thus, it can be used by a fieldworker who is studying the effect of sociocultural conditions on his subjects. He can contrast subjects who show high stress with those who show little stress and draw conclusions as to which sociocultural factors may be related to the difference between them. But he cannot use the HOS to diagnose the condition of any person. In Leighton's pioneer study in "Stirling County," the levels of stress were found to be correlated (among other things) with levels of community disorganization; that is, the communities in the county that no longer had intact traditional organizations and relationships showed significantly higher levels of stress than those which still had a distinct organization.

Similar results were found by the Leighton group in a very different cultural environment, namely among the Yoruba of Nigeria. In both cases, members of disorganized groups showed many symptoms of reaction to stress, sometimes amounting to mental or emotional disturbance that could be confirmed by clinicians. Thus, the HOS has been utilized cross-culturally, to the extent that it has been shown to measure stress levels in at least two different cultures. It can be shown to correlate with a number of other sociocultural factors in addition to the one discussed.

It should be kept in mind that no survey, no matter how carefully standardized, will be perfectly appropriate in every cultural situation. The researcher thus has an obligation to determine if any parts of the standardized survey would be either offensive or meaningless to the people being studied, another good reason to delay the administration of such a test until the fieldworker has a deeper, more personal knowledge of the culture.

THE PROJECT

The general hypothesis that social stress is reflected in physiological symptoms has been tested in several cultural settings, but the more supportive data we can collect from more varied communities, the more our understanding will grow. Do not feel, therefore, that you are merely repeating something that has already been done. Even on a very small scale, this project can be a meaningful contribution to the cross-cultural understanding of the relationship between social structure and personality function.

Please note that the concept of "stress" is one which is the subject of much discussion among behavioral and medical scientists. Our discussion here is not meant to imply that "stress" is a clear-cut "thing" about which everyone would agree. It is for this reason that we use the Leighton concept for illustration. It would be meaningless in any culture (including our own) to ask someone, "What gives you stress?" It is better to focus on the perceived appearance of a variety of general symptoms that collectively indicate some sort of feeling of unease or ill health, a feeling that, for convenience, we can label "stress."

The first step is to select a community for study. Preferably it should be one with which you have worked in other projects, so that you have some familiarity with the people and some knowledge of their patterns of behavior. In any case, the community selected should be one that is small enough to enable you to survey most of its members efficiently in a relatively short time, and yet large enough to show a range of age, sex, occupation, educational background, religion, or whatever other social variables you care to consider. If you are working with an on-campus population, you might, for example, restrict yourself to residents of one floor in a dorm, or members of a large lecture section in a required course, or all the people holding regular meal tickets in a dining hall. If you are working off campus, let yourself be guided by the amount of territory you can reasonably cover: one large apartment house, one city block, or a clearly defined neighborhood. A more elaborate survey, covering many sectors of a larger community, can, of course, be made by doing the project as a team effort, with a division of labor clearly established beforehand to avoid duplication.

It is frequently necessary when administering survey questionnaires to select a representative sample of a larger "universe." For example, if we want to determine the effects of stress among adult American males, it would obviously be impossible to survey each and every one of them.

Methods have been devised to enable the researcher to select only a portion of that total, but to select individuals whose answers will in some way be statistically representative of the whole group. Since this project asks you only to choose a very small, well-bounded, easily surveyed population, you need not worry about such statistical refinements. Nor need you be concerned with the fact that most researchers pretest a questionnaire in a sample population in order to be able to discard useless questions, add questions that get at attitudes not previously thought of, and the like. Since the HOS has been standardized for use cross-culturally, we can assume that all of its questions will fit almost any cultural situation. More advanced students, however, who are interested in preparing their own questionnaires, should be aware of these and other related problems. A handy reference is *Epidemiologic Methods* [MacMahon, Pugh, & Ipsen 1960], which deals with data collection and methods of analysis in the health sciences.

One of the basic principles of ethnographic fieldwork is that the anthropologist establishes a "special relationship" with his informants. The rapport that exists between them means that he can elicit information in a friendly atmosphere that will enhance cooperation. It is usually unwise to launch a field study with the administration of a standardized test that must be administered in a somewhat formal way and thus can put a certain distance between the questioner and his subject. It is, therefore, a good idea to put off any test until a working relationship has been established, such that the informant will trust his new friend's intentions. When administering the HOS, the interviewer can start off with the collection of background information about the subject, having already found out who he is and where he fits into the community. If, however, there are any gaps in his knowledge about the informant, this often provides a good opportunity to collect general census information. At any rate, the role of the impersonal pollster ringing the doorbells of perfect strangers and immediately asking impertinent questions is emphatically *not* the proper role for an anthropologist.

The HOS can be administered by the anthropologist, who reads the questions word for word, in the proper order. If the subject is fully literate, he can mark the answers himself. If the fieldworker is dealing with informants who speak another language, and if he himself is not fully bilingual, it is best to work with a bilingual informant beforehand and agree upon a standard translation of the questions that conveys the original meaning in the language of the subjects. Administering the questionnaire is like taking a medical history—we really want to ask the questions in a way the subject will understand and that will provide standardized information that can be compared to data collected in other administrations of the questionnaire. *Exactly the same words* (whatever they are) should be used with all subjects in a given group.

The twenty questions and the scores for their responses are:*

1. Do you have any physical or health problems at the present?
   3. Yes _____   1. No _____

2. Do your hands tremble enough to bother you?
   3. Often _____   2. Sometimes _____   1. Never _____

3. Are you troubled by your hands or feet sweating so that they feel damp and clammy?
   3. Often _____   2. Sometimes _____   1. Never _____

4. Are you bothered by your heart beating hard?
   3. Often _____   2. Sometimes _____   1. Never _____

5. Do you tend to feel tired in the morning?
   3. Often _____   2. Sometimes _____   1. Never _____

6. Do you have any trouble getting to sleep or staying asleep?
   3. Often _____   2. Sometimes _____   1. Never _____

7. How often are you bothered by having an upset stomach?
   3. Often _____   2. Sometimes _____   1. Never _____

8. Are you bothered by nightmares (dreams that frighten or upset you)?
   3. Often _____   2. Sometimes _____   1. Never _____

9. Are you troubled by "cold sweats"?
   3. Often _____   2. Sometimes _____   1. Never _____

10. Do you feel that you are bothered by all sorts (different kinds) of ailments in different parts of your body?
   3. Often _____   2. Sometimes _____   1. Never _____

11. Do you smoke?
   3. Often _____   2. Sometimes _____   1. Never _____

12. Do you have loss of appetite?
   3. Often _____   2. Sometimes _____   1. Never _____

13. Does ill health affect the amount of work (or housework) that you do?
   3. Often _____   2. Sometimes _____   1. Never _____

14. Do you feel weak all over?
   3. Often _____   2. Sometimes _____   1. Never _____

*We are grateful to Dr. Dorothea C. Leighton, University of North Carolina, for permission to reprint the Health Opinion Survey.

15. Do you have spells of dizziness?

    3. Often _____   2. Sometimes _____   1. Never _____

16. Do you tend to lose weight when you worry?

    3. Often _____   2. Sometimes _____   1. Never _____

17. Are you bothered by shortness of breath when you are not exerting yourself?

    3. Often _____   2. Sometimes _____   1. Never _____

18. Do you feel healthy enough to carry out the things that you would like to do?

    1. Often _____   2. Sometimes _____   3. Never _____

19. Do you feel in good spirits?

    1. Often _____   2. Sometimes _____   3. Never _____

20. Do you sometimes wonder if anything is worthwhile any more?

    3. Often _____   2. Sometimes _____   1. Never _____

The score is obtained by summing the numbers in front of the answers the subject selects. These twenty questions, obviously, measure only stress. Sociocultural factors with which to correlate the score have to be obtained by other means, such as the "census" questions, and whatever else it is desired to investigate.

Hypotheses regarding the relationships that will be found should be stated before the study as educated guesses regarding the probable factors that will be found to be related to high or low stress.

It is important that the informant choose his own answer. It helps to remind him that there is no right answer, and that he is the only person who knows the answer that is appropriate for him. Most subjects enjoy talking about their symptoms, especially if good rapport has been established from the start. Occasionally, the best strategy is for the researcher to get the subject to tell anecdotally about his experiences with such symptoms, after which the researcher can make his own judgment as to whether the subject has experienced this symptom often, sometimes, or never. This is all too often a wild guess, however, and not good technique. Remember, too, that what is important is what the informant *believes* to be true, not whether a doctor would agree with him. For example, in one field situation, a man whom the anthropologist knew very well to be a hearty eater responded very definitely that he "often" had loss of appetite. This probably indicated that the man felt himself to have lost his appetite, although an observer would not have noticed it. Thus, the response tells us that he was, indeed, feeling some kind of stress, even though it was not a "true" response in the objective sense.

When all the tests have been administered, the scores may be grouped thus:

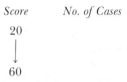

Score   No. of Cases

20

↓

60

Scores of 20 to 29 are considered within the normal limits; 30 to 34 show a borderline stress level; 35+ is considered "too much stress." One should not, however, take these as absolute limits. A person with a score of 35 is not significantly more disturbed than someone with a 34, nor is a person with a high score necessarily "sick."

However, what emerges from this distribution of scores is a preliminary picture of what is associated with stress in the community under study. We can now identify those people showing different levels of stress and study their characteristics. It is at this point that we can begin to analyze the results and try to explain the distribution. The researcher can thus select any social factors that he suspects might be implicated in the creation of stress in this group, on the basis of his knowledge of the community. If the group is heterogeneous with regard to religion, occupation, educational level, and so forth, each of these categories can be tested against the level of stress. For example, it would be a common finding in "modern" societies that the largest number of high HOS scores is associated with subjects with only a primary education, and the largest number of low HOS scores is associated with subjects who are college graduates. A simple χ^2 (chi-square) test may be useful in determining the significance of these correlations.

STRESS

Educational Level	High (35+)	Medium (30–34)	Low (20–29)
	(number of cases per category)		
College Graduate			
High School Graduate			
Primary School			

It is likely that in any one community only a few factors will show a statistically significant correlation with the level of stress. On the basis of your field experience in this society, you should be able to suggest reasons why this (these) factor(s) seem to be so important in this particular setting. A brief discussion of such observational data should accompany the tabular report of your survey.

The HOS can be used in other ways to refine hypotheses such as those discussed above. For example, questions 2, 3, 4, 8, 9, and 17 can be scored separately to get a measure of feelings of *anxiety,* while numbers 5, 13, 16, 18, 19, and 20 measure feelings of *depression.* Anxiety and depression are, of course, two common components of the overall stress syndrome. These subscores can be tallied separately and correlated independently with the social variables you have chosen in order to determine whether a particular type of symptom is more highly correlated with certain social factors than with others. You should write a brief summary explaining the sociocultural reasons for whatever correlations seem to make good sense, whether or not they are statistically significant.

SELECTED ANNOTATED BIBLIOGRAPHY

Benedict, Ruth
> *Patterns of Culture.* Houghton Mifflin, 1959. The classic study of cultural norms and the role of the deviant in society, it was originally published in 1934, and is available in many subsequent editions.

Cameron, N. A.
> *Personality Development and Psychopathology: A Dynamic Approach.* Houghton Mifflin, 1963. Some good background material, particularly on anxiety and depression as manifestations of mental disturbance.

Du Bois, Cora
> *People of Alor.* University of Minnesota Press, 1944. A classic "psychocultural" ethnography that made use of a number of standardized measuring techniques (not the HOS, however).

Hallowell, A. Irving
> *Culture and Experience.* University of Pennsylvania Press, 1955. A collection of essays on standardized methods for measuring stress, particularly that resulting from the acculturation process.

Hughes, Charles C., et al.
> *People of Cove and Woodlot.* Basic Books, 1960. The summary of ethnographic data of the Stirling County Study.

Langley, Russell
> *Practical Statistics for Non-Mathematical People.* Drake Publishers, 1971. If you need some extra information about, or practice in, statistical methods, this is a painless source.

Leighton, Alexander H.
> *My Name Is Legion.* Basic Books, 1959. The theoretical background of the Stirling County Study.

Leighton, Alexander H., et al.
> *Psychiatric Disorder Among the Yoruba.* Cornell University Press, 1963. An account of the cross-cultural pilot study by the Cornell team.

Leighton, Dorothea C., et al.
> *The Character of Danger.* Basic Books, 1963. The summary of psychiatric data and their sociocultural correlates from the Stirling County study.

MacMahon, Brian, Thomas F. Pugh, and Johannes Ipsen
> *Epidemiologic Methods.* Little, Brown, 1960. A survey of statistical and other methodological approaches to the study of health behavior.

Macmillan, A. M.
> *The Health Opinion Survey: Technique for Estimating Prevalence of Psychoneurotic and Related Types of Disorder in Communities.* Grand Forks, North Dakota: Southern Universities Press, 1957, Psychological Reports 3 (Monograph Supplement 7): 325–329. A brief account of the history of the HOS and an analysis of its proper use.

Mechanic, David
> *Students Under Stress.* The Free Press, 1962. An extensive study of the social factors involved in stress among a group of Ph.D. candidates.

Mechanic, David
> *Medical Sociology: A Selective View.* The Free Press, 1968. An exposition of the theory underlying much of the contemporary work in medical behavioral science.

Miller, Delbert
> *Handbook of Research Design and Social Measurement.* McKay, 1964. A concise compilation of behavioral science surveys and tests.

Selye, Hans
> *The Stress of Life.* McGraw-Hill, 1956. The classic study of stress and its effects on physical and mental health.

Siegel, Sidney
> *Nonparametric Statistics for the Behavioral Sciences.* McGraw-Hill, 1956. Another useful source book in statistical methods as applied in the social sciences.

Spindler, George
> *Sociocultural and Psychological Processes in Menomini Acculturation.* University of California Publications in Culture and Society, V, 1955. A standard work describing the use of projective tests in the study of individuals and their cultural backgrounds.

PROJECT TWELVE

STUDYING FORMAL ORGANIZATIONS

INTRODUCTION

Sociologists have been the social scientists most typically concerned with studying such formalized aspects of social structure as "bureaucracies" or "organizational institutions." But anthropologists, too, have been aware of the fact that the technologically primitive, traditionally organized societies that they often studied had formal institutions as well. Such organizations, of course, did not have written bylaws, and, more often than not, they were based on ties of kinship and ritual.

Studies of African kingdoms by British anthropologists, for example, have shown quite clearly that elaborate bureaucracies can exist even in nonliterate, technologically primitive societies [Fortes & Evans-Pritchard 1940]. Similarly, a traditional, religiously oriented collection of people and behaviors, as in the caste system of village India, could be viewed as if it were similar in nature to the apparently more formal organizations of Western society [Cohn 1971, Chap. 11].

In fact, one of the classic principles of social anthropology (referring broadly to the British, as opposed to the American, school of anthropology) has been the concept of "corporate" organizations. [See Beattie 1964, Chap. 7, for a discussion of this and other related principles of British social anthropology.] Although there has been much confusion in the use of this concept [Dow 1973], we may say that a lineage, clan, village, or some other apparently "informal" or kin-based traditional group in a non-Western society can be analyzed as if it were something like a corporation in the Western world of business and finance. For example, in the traditional Indian village, the principal mark of wealth and social rank was land, which was owned by the joint family—a group of men and their wives living in the house of the men's father. Because the land was theoretically a joint, or corporate, property, no one individual in the family had the right to dispose of it, or, in fact, to do anything to, with, or on it without first seeking the permission of the others. Thus, the specific individual was not so important because "the family" would continue to own the land after he had died, just as it had before he was ever born. In the same way, the Western corporation would continue regardless of which individuals at any one moment comprised the board of directors. The old patriarch, like the chairman of the board, may have had more power in deciding matters about the common property; but, theoretically at least, he could not be arbitrary about it, since it was not really his to deal with [Mandelbaum 1970; Orenstein 1956, Chap. 3].

To be sure, the Indian joint family is not precisely like a Western corporation, since its members are neither selected to fill their positions nor are they kept in their positions by receiving specific salaries. Moreover, there are no definite bylaws to guide the day-to-day operation of the family. Instead, people are members of the family "corporation" because of kinship ties, and are kept in their positions by various types of mutual ritual obligations. Their "bylaws" or "company charters" are to be found only in very general form in the ancient moral treatises of the Hindu tradition.

But, although the bases for establishing the corporate family unit are different from those generating the formal corporation in our society, the two may, in fact, be studied in the same ways, in part by reference to the linked concepts of status and role.

The concepts of status and role, although employed most characteristically by sociologists, were given their first major discussion by anthropologists interested in the study of social structure in a wide variety of societies in different parts of the world.

In commonsense usage, the term "status" often implies prestige or rank, as when we say, "His new job gives him a lot of status." In the social science definition, however, statuses are found even in societies that are not marked by true hierarchical organization. A status, then, has been defined as "a collection of rights and duties" [Linton 1936, p. 113]. In other words, to say that a man is a "father" is to refer to one cluster of rights and duties that defines his "fatherly" position in relation to other individuals. Being a father, then, means occupying a particular status. Clearly, then, all members of a society will have many statuses over the course of their lifetimes and will, in fact, occupy many statuses simultaneously. A man is not only someone's father; he is, at the same time, someone else's son, and someone else's husband. In addition, he may be a teacher, boss, employee. One may be born into one of these categories (*ascribed status*), such as one's sex, race, ethnic group. One may fit into other groups later in life on the basis of merit or attainment (*achieved status*). An individual's place in his society is, therefore, the sum total of all the statuses he occupies. To be sure, many statuses are ranked. The status of school principal is higher than that of teacher; being a father carries more authority than being a son, and so forth. But this ranking need not be rigid. An individual who ranks high in one interaction (as a principal in relation to the teachers on his staff) will be subservient in another situation (when, for example, he is a member of a church congregation and defers to the minister).

> The relation between any individual and any status he holds is somewhat like that between the driver of an automobile and the driver's place in the machine. The driver's seat with its steering wheel, accelerator, and other controls is a constant with ever-present potentialities for action and control, while the driver may be any member of the family and may exercise these potentialities very well or very badly [Linton 1936, p. 113].

A study of the statuses involved in any given social situation can yield much valuable information about the way in which a community is organized. But the anthropologist is often concerned not only with the formal, ideal structural framework, but with the real behaviors that people in a society exhibit. The behaviors associated with statuses are known as roles. "When [an individual] puts the rights and duties which constitute the status into effect, he is performing a rôle" [Linton 1936, p. 114]. In many ways, role behavior is patterned and formalized, as every society will have certain approved ways of acting in any given situation. However, just as an actor has some leeway in interpreting his role in a play, so individuals in any society have a certain amount of freedom in acting out the several roles that are characteristic of any status.

Thus, there are certain things that we, in our society, think of as being appropriate fatherly behavior, and we would be likely to criticize any man who deviated outrageously from these norms. But, within the range of acceptable fatherly behavior, there may be as many variants as there are individuals in one's observed sample. For these reasons, the anthropologist studies statuses in order to discover how interpersonal relationships are structured in any given society; he studies roles in order to understand the ongoing dynamics of social interaction. He can then compare both the ideal and the real activities of people from one society to another, and thereby gain a better understanding of the cultural process. Culture, it should be remembered, is not a machine that rigidly molds all its members into one pattern of conformity. Culture may limit activity in some ways, but, since it is a growing, changing, open-ended system of behaviors and attitudes, it must always allow for variability. Although expressions of ideal behavior represent the "musts" and "shoulds" of a culture, there seem to be different levels of working them out in reality. Beals and Hoijer (quoting Kluckhohn) point out that there are five categories of ideal behavior:

- compulsory (only one proper thing to do in a given situation)
- preferred (several acceptable choices, but one considered better than the rest)
- typical (several acceptable choices, but one is expressed more frequently than the rest)
- alternative (several acceptable choices, with no difference in either value or frequency of expression)
- restricted (ways of behaving which are proper for only some, not all, members of society) [Beals & Hoijer 1953, p. 213]

It is clear that the organization of statuses and roles will be somewhat different in different types of societies. There will be a great concentration of statuses in the so-called "primitive" or "simple" societies. For example, in a small hunting and gathering band, the same man who is your mother's brother is also your father-in-law and may also be a shaman who cures your illness, the leader of the hunting party that secures your food, the headman who leads you on a raid against enemies, the artisan who fashions your arrows, and so forth. In "complex" societies, on the other hand, it would be very rare for one's father, doctor, lawyer, congressman, teacher, and boss to be the same person. Clearly, then, understanding the organization of these statuses can tell us a great deal about the qualitative aspects of life in a society. Thus, interpersonal relationships in a "primitive" society may actually be more complex than in our own because there are so many levels on which two individuals may be interacting with each other. In our society, such interactions are more near-ly individualized.

Statuses must be paired in order to be meaningful; this is known as a *dyadic* relationship. For example, the status of "fa-ther" is meaningless without the corresponding status of "son," or "daughter." The personnel of the various dyads may shift, as in the case of a man who is a "son" to an older man or woman, but who is a "father" to a little boy or girl. That one man, then, is a member of two different dyadic relationships with two or more different individuals. Yet on the structural, more abstract level, the relationships are the same; there are father (mother) – son (daughter) dyads. We can then talk about the abstract status dyad of father-son, for example, and, in studying a culture, we would attempt to discover what the components of such a pair-ing would be. An ethnographer in the field would observe the many different real examples of this abstract dyad in order to see what sorts of role behaviors fall into the acceptable range of variation for the several observed fathers and sons, and which are disapproved of. In the latter case, we could also attempt to discern *why* the observed behaviors are not approved.

The learning of statuses and roles by members of a given community is part of the process that sociologists term *socializa-tion*. Anthropologists use a related term, *enculturation*, to deal with the same phenomena. There are technical differences be-tween the two concepts, but the two terms can be treated as virtually synonymous for all practical purposes.

Although it has become customary to restrict discussions of socialization or enculturation to the area of child development, it is also possible to discuss this process with regard to adults. Every time an individual in any culture enters into a new social situation, he must be socialized. This means that he must learn what the new status entails and what sorts of role behaviors are to be associated with it. In many cultures, certain highly signifi-cant changes in status are marked by *rites of passage*, elaborate rituals that mark a public confirmation of the fact that an indi-vidual has undertaken a new set of relationships [Beals & Hoijer 1953, p. 497]. In our society, we do not necessarily hold public feasts when we take new jobs; but there is a socialization in that new position as well. It is somewhat difficult to study the sociali-zation of any individual into an informal dyadic relationship: the question of how one initiates a new friendship, for example, has been very little studied by social scientists. But when we deal with formal organizations, in which the process is made explicit (even if it is not commonly thought of as a socialization process like those that children undergo), we can get a much better understanding of how members of a particular society conceptualize ideal relationships, how they define "proper" behavior, and what leeway they are permitted in working out the relationships in question.

Therefore, whether one chooses to do fieldwork in a traditional culture or in our own society, the study of organizations can be of value in aiding the understanding of the ways in which individuals fit into larger units, the society or the culture—a basic concern of both sociology and anthropology, we might add. On the basis of the foregoing discussion, we can use the following basic criteria for delineating a "formal" organization for the purposes of this project:

- it must be a group which transcends its individual members (that is, it must be something that will have some degree of continuity regardless of shifts in personnel)
- it must have a system of defined statuses recognized by at least the members of the group, and possibly also by outsiders
- it must have some sort of charter (written or not, but including some means of sanctioning behavior—either of rewarding conformity to accepted behavior, or of punishing deviance from it) that aids its members in defining their proper role behaviors
- it must have a regularized means of initiating new members into the group, and of conveying to them their new place, and the behaviors that will be expected of them

The study of formal organizations is an increasingly important interest among anthropologists. In most parts of the world, the processes variously labelled "modernization" or "development" often include the formalization of social institutions along lines more nearly like the bureaucracies of the Western world. For example, there is some evidence to indicate that as the ancient village system of India changes, the once ritually organized caste-system groups are becoming formalized and are acting as political parties on the national level [Cohn 1971, pp. 129–130]. Therefore, by using some of the concepts borrowed from the studies of social organization among "traditional" peoples, contemporary anthropologists can bring the continuity of their anthropological perspective to the study of modern or modernizing societies.

A concrete example may help clarify these issues. Alcoholics

Anonymous is an internationally recognized organization founded in 1935 by the late "Bill W.," an alcoholic stockbroker, with the aid of a psychiatrist and a religious counselor. The essential core of the program has never changed, based as it is on Bill's example of successful "recovery" (note that according to A.A., one is never "cured" of alcoholism; and, although one may "recover" from the effects of the disease, the victim is always at risk of a relapse unless he or she follows the program rigorously). Bill's principles are embodied in what the members call the "Twelve-by-Twelve," the Twelve Steps and Twelve Traditions. The Twelve Steps are the things the individual alcoholic must do to repair his personal life and thereby maintain his sobriety, while the Twelve Traditions are the guidelines that the A.A. groups follow in order to maintain the "fellowship" deemed necessary for the individual's recovery. In addition to the "Twelve-by-Twelve," A.A. publishes the "Big Book," which includes several more detailed discussions of the A.A. principles and way of life, analyses of the program by medical, psychiatric, and religious experts, and personal testimonies by recovering alcoholics.

These books, plus the numerous other books, pamphlets, tapes, and films that form the basic A.A. literature disseminated from the General Service Office in New York City, form the basis of the formal, ideal A.A. program. They therefore constitute the ideal charter of every A.A. group everywhere in the world. According to this charter, there are to be no "bosses" within the group, as each member is equal to all the others. There are, however, certain positions that are to be filled, lest the group dissolve into chaos: each group has a chairperson who is responsible for calling the meeting to order, calling speakers during a meeting, seeing that speakers stick to time limits, and planning any special events or projects on behalf of the group. There is also a secretary in charge of correspondence and taking minutes (in larger groups the corresponding and recording secretaries might be different individuals), and a treasurer who collects donations. Each A.A. group is expected to be self-supporting through the donations of its members. These donations are used, in part, to buy coffee and other refreshments served at the meetings, and in some groups there is a separate office of "coffee man," responsible for securing and seeing to the refreshments. These officers, however, are considered to be "servants of the people," and are not supposed to abuse their authority by acting like bosses. Even members who have been in the group for many years, who know more about alcoholism and are better at public speaking and interpreting the literature, are considered merely "elder statesmen," who are expected to offer advice but never to issue orders. Newcomers are made aware of all of this as they listen to the speakers; the new members are not required to say anything or take part in the meeting until they are ready to stand up and say, "My name is . . . and I am an alcoholic." Thus, not until they have assimilated the proper concepts of status and role in the group will they become functioning members of the group.

Thus, A.A. is a formal organization in the sense that:

- it is a group with a continuous tradition that has included many individuals through the years;
- it has a specific charter that states the purposes, aims, and methods of the group;
- it has a recognized set of statuses, each with a specific set of behaviors considered to be appropriate to the position, and a formal method of socializing newcomers to those positions.

A.A. has had great success, not only among members of different classes and racial and ethnic groups in the United States, but in other countries as well. In general, this success is due to the highly adaptable nature of the A.A. organization, which can change in various ways to become acceptable in different societies even without changing the basic "message" of recovery.

For example, A.A. was introduced on the island of Trinidad in the West Indies a little more than a decade ago. Although it has certainly not eliminated the very extensive problem of alcoholism there, it has been quite successful. There are now approximately forty different groups operating in villages scattered over the island. Interestingly enough, virtually the entire membership of the Trinidad A.A. consists of people of East Indian descent. People from India were brought to certain parts of the Caribbean area, beginning in 1837, as indentured laborers who were imported as plantation workers following the emancipation of the slaves. They now form one-third to one-half the population of Trinidad, but have often been considered more traditional and less Westernized than the black people of the island. It might seem unlikely that A.A., which was developed by a middle-class white man in the United States, and which relies on Christian teachings, would have much appeal to the relatively non-Westernized Hindu or Muslim Indians. Nevertheless, although the charter, as embodied in the "Twelve-by-Twelve" and the other official writings, remains the ideal, the A.A. groups on the island have, in reality a somewhat different conception of the arrangement of statuses and their associated role behaviors.

Thus, while the concept of equality and "no bosses" is invoked as an ideal tradition by the members of the Trinidad A.A., many of the groups there are constructed quite explicitly, with one member (always a man) gaining sobriety and then gathering a core of disciples around him. This man is known as the "sponsor" of all the others whom he brings into the group. A person's "sponsor" in A.A. is owed a great deal of loyalty; and if two sponsors quarrel, their respective supporters will line up into opposing factions. It is often said that the first step in the backsliding process, by which a member gives up the A.A. program and begins drinking again, is the member's defiance of his sponsor's right to call on his loyalty. This type of organization, which seems on the surface to be so foreign to the A.A. ideal, is really a reflection of the typical sociopolitical situation in the rural Indian villages of Trinidad. There, the heads of lineages would form a council of village elders (the *panchayat*, formerly a caste council in India itself). Although the elders would theoretically work together to plan for the village as a whole, they often disagreed with one another, and factions would arise as each elder called upon his immediate followers to support him. In many ways, of course, this was disruptive and counterproductive; but, since this was the way in which the Indians typically conceptualized authority figures, it would be easier for them to accept the authority of the A.A. teachings if the latter were presented by leaders who behaved in the expected leader-like manner.

Nevertheless, the *jefes* (a borrowed Spanish word meaning "chief," which is applied to the most influential sponsors) are seldom the chairmen of their groups, as they prefer to be "preachers" who give lengthy, moralistic sermons at the meetings. The chairman, then, becomes very much like the *pandit* or *imam* (the Hindu or Muslim priest, respectively). In Trinidad, these priests are generally ritual functionaries, and only a few of them maintain the reputation that they have in India for being great scholars, teachers, or ascetics. One calls a priest in Trinidad to perform a service: to purify one's house, for example, or to induct one's children into adult status within the religion. The *pandits* and *imams* thus have the force of moral authority behind them, but are seldom real powers in their communities, in part because they are only part-time specialists, and often work at nonreligious jobs to earn their livings. The chairman of the group, then, takes on a sort of priestly air. When he rises to begin the meeting, silence descends on the room; and he leads the group in reciting the "A.A. Serenity Prayer" (or he designates someone in the congregation to do so). The A.A. meeting itself is highly ritualized. Members favor the technique of repeating selected passages from the A.A. literature when they gave their "contributions," much as Hindu devotees repeat *mantras*, or phrases from the sacred texts. The order of the program is considered inviolate—the group strives to do everything in the same order every time it meets, and deviations from the expected order are met with disconcerted mutterings by the audience.

According to A.A. tradition, Bill W. and his friends formed the first A.A. group while drinking coffee; and, in fact, the coffee pot in which Bill's wife brewed the first "A.A. coffee" is on display in Bill's home, now a museum. The Trinidadians have elevated the coffee break at meetings to a position of great ceremonial importance. At Hindu rituals, the climax of the service is known as the sharing of the *parsad*, or the distribution of blessed offerings of food. The A.A. coffee break is very much like the *parsad* distribution: the chairman very formally asks the "coffee man" (who is very much like the *pandit*'s apprentice) to serve the refreshments, an act which he almost always describes as "sharing the fellowship." Members who leave before the coffee break are chided for "missing the fellowship," even if they have heard all the contributions. The coffee break is also the time at which a sponsor introduces his latest protege to the group; the latter is expected to play a subservient role, as a student among teachers, until he is ready to "make the admission." As with the ritual *parsad*, the coffee break refreshments seldom vary from the approved food, in this case coffee and biscuits; other foods are considered inappropriate.

It is clear that the Trinidad A.A. members have shifted the arrangement of statuses within the group. They have also changed their behavior at meetings, and they have an attitude toward the program and its procedures that is distinctly different from that of a typical American member. However, it is often easier to introduce a radically new ideology if it is presented in the guise of comfortable, familiar forms. Although the Trinidad A.A. members have not done so consciously, their ability to make their own reality out of the ideal A.A. structure of statuses and roles has made them pioneers in bringing a new belief system to their communities.

THE PROJECT

Using the general criteria for the formal organization discussed above, select a group with which you are already reasonably familiar on the "ideal" level. A good example might be a political group that has a well-known philosophy and organizational structure. Obviously, one of the national parties is too big an entity to study conveniently, but the major parties often have local offices or "clubs" in various areas. You could then compare the ideal philosophy and organizational structure of the national party (as expressed in the platform it adopted in the most recent general election, for example) with the actual ways in which the local club works. Your observations of the club may, if you choose, take the form suggested for the participant observation approach in Project 5. However, you should be thinking of some or all of the following questions more specifically:

- What are the different statuses represented in this group, according to its charter (e.g., chairman, vice-chairman, secretary, treasurer, social chairman, research assistant, etc..)? Are all of them represented in the local club?

- In what ways are the different statuses associated with different behaviors (roles)? What should a chairman do according to the ideal charter? What does he really do? Remember to define each status in terms of the rights and duties associated with it vis-à-vis the other people in the group.

- If more than one person fills a certain status (e.g., telephone canvassers during an election) what are the variants in their role behaviors? In what ways does the group signal its belief that one or more of the individuals has overstepped the bounds of accepted variation within that role?

- If you can observe it, how is a newcomer socialized into his new status and role?

Your report should include a brief statement of the "ideal" status and role organization of the group, as expressed in its "charter" (whatever that might turn out to be). The main part of the report, however, should be your description of the way in which the group you are observing works. You may also try to analyze *why* the group under study indulges in "real" behavior that is somehow different from its expected ideal. It should be clearly stated that the aim of comparing ideal behavior with real behavior is *not* to prove that a given set of people is either deceitful or foolish. The purpose of such a study is to better understand how culture works as a dynamic system — to understand the boundaries that are set on individual behavior and the ways in which individuals choose to work out their permitted variations of behavior. By studying the formal organization, we can get an explicit statement of the boundaries of appropriate behavior (as expressed in the "ideal" charter), the better to analyze the real behavior that we have observed in the field. Although we can obtain rich ethnographic data by observing the day-to-day activity of a political club, for instance, we would not really know very much about the sociocultural system in which that club operated unless we were aware of the formal boundaries of expectation in which the members of that club were performing their duties.

If you do not have access to a political club, or if studying one would pose too many ethical problems for you, you may select any group at all, as long as it meets the broad criteria discussed above. Virtually any fraternity/sorority, academic, or social club on campus will fit the bill, as all are generally required to have formal charters on file with the college administration, charters that may or may not be strictly adhered to in actual behavior.

SELECTED ANNOTATED BIBLIOGRAPHY

Alcoholics Anonymous
    Alcoholics Anonymous. Works Publishers, 1950. The "Big Book," the compendium of official AA literature: case histories of alcoholics, analyses by psychological, medical, and religious authorities, and outlines of the A.A. program.
Alcoholics Anonymous
    Twelve Steps and Twelve Traditions. Alcoholics Anonymous Publishing, 1963. An annotated survey of the steps which the individual alcoholic uses in his personal recovery and of the traditions which guide A.A. groups.
Angrosino, Michael V.
    Alcoholism, Ideology and Community Organization Among the East Indians of Trinidad. Wake Forest University, Medical Behavioral Science Monograph Series of the Overseas Research Center, 1974. An extended analysis of the Trinidad A.A. materials discussed in this chapter.
Beals, Ralph L., and Harry Hoijer
    An Introduction to Anthropology. Macmillan, 1953. A well-known introductory text that has some very clear presentations of the concepts discussed in this chapter.
Beattie, John
    Other Cultures. London: Cohen and West, 1964. A frequently cited introduction to the concepts of British social anthropology.
Burling, Temple, Edith M. Lentz, and Robert N. Wilson
    The Give and Take in Hospitals: A Study of Human Organization in Hospitals.

Putnam, 1956. A pioneering study of the hospital as a formal social system. The study of hospitals and other institutions (including prisons) has since become one of the major interests of both sociologists and anthropologists.

Chalmers, D. M.

Hooded Americanism: The First Century of the Ku Klux Klan 1865–1965. Doubleday, 1965. An interesting account of a contemporary political and social group in our own society.

Cohn, Bernard S.

India: The Social Anthropology of a Civilization. Prentice-Hall, 1971. A concise ethnography, cited here because of its discussion of the organization of the Indian family.

Dow, James

"On the Muddled Concept of Corporation in Anthropology." *American Anthropologist,* 1973, 75:904–908. A critical review of the uses of this classic social anthropological principle.

Fortes, Meyer, and E.E. Evans-Pritchard, eds.

African Political Systems. International African Institute (Oxford University Press), 1940. A classic work of British social anthropology, cited here for its comparative discussion of political organizations in some African societies.

Gellman, Irving Peter

The Sober Alcoholic: An Organizational Analysis of A.A. College and University Press, 1964. A detailed account of an American A.A. group's "real" behavior analyzed within the context of the A.A. "ideal." This study analyzes an American group in much the same manner as the Trinidad study suggests.

Keiser, R. Lincoln

The Vice Lords: Warriors of the Streets. Holt, Rinehart and Winston, 1969. The ethnography of an urban street gang, another example of the varieties of formal organizations being studied by contemporary social scientists.

Linton, Ralph

The Study of Man. Appleton-Century, 1936. Contains what is generally regarded as the classic statement of the anthropological concepts of status and role.

Mandelbaum, David G.

Society in India. 2 vols., University of California Press, 1970. A detailed ethnography of India, cited here for its discussion of family and village organization.

Orenstein, Henry M.

Gaon: Conflict and Cohesion in an Indian Village. Princeton University Press, 1965. An ethnography of an Indian village, illustrating the principles of corporate organization in a non-Western society.

PROJECT THIRTEEN

TAKING PHOTOGRAPHS

INTRODUCTION

No matter what one's mental image of the modern anthropological fieldworker might be, we expect to see a camera hanging somewhere on the person of the anthropologist busily doing his or her "thing."

Louis Daguerre perfected the first light-sensitive plate in 1837, and his daguerreotypes introduced photography to the world. Even in the earliest periods of photography, when the subjects had their heads held by vises and had to remain achingly immobile for the long spaces of time necessary to take a photograph, more than 95 per cent of all daguerreotypes made in the United States were portraits of individuals, couples, or groups [Rudisill 1971, p. 198]. Early writings about photography stress the idea that photographs can confer a form of immortality, and a sitter can be held forever before a loving eye. Obviously, throughout the history of photography, then, it is not only anthropologists who have felt that "the proper study of mankind is man." The timeless appeal of pictures of people is well illustrated by popular collections such as *The Family of Man* [1955], once a travelling exhibition and now a much-reprinted book, and by the liberally illustrated book *Family* [1965], which combines the anthropological talents of Margaret Mead with the superb photography of Ken Heyman.

Although an occasional enterprising anthropological fieldworker ventured to take a recording machine or camera into the field several decades ago, it is only in the past few decades that these mechanisms have become indispensable equipment for most ethnographers. As equipment has become more portable, more flexible, and adaptable to a variety of research situations, easier to protect from extreme climatic conditions, and—in simpler forms, at least—easier to afford, increasing numbers of anthropologists have done increasing amounts of photography in the field, many of them developing their own films as well. A few innovative projects have used members of the society being studied as the photographers, thereby gaining valuable insights into how people view and represent their own society and culture.

The camera "sees" differently than does the human eye. When our photographs are printed, we see not only what we were culturally conditioned to see in the fraction of a second when the picture was taken, but also the totality of social interaction and material culture that was present within the scope of the camera's lens. In a photograph, myriad relationships and details are held in timelessness for our later inspection, and for use by others. The photograph allows for a more comprehensive record than any verbal description could give, and acts as a control factor for descriptions made from visual observations.

Like other data, photographs reflect the inherent biases of the researcher. The decision as to what constitutes an important enough moment or subject to warrant a picture is influenced not only by the purposes of the research at hand. It is influenced also by the cultural conditioning of the person behind the lens, as a comparison between a sequence of photographs taken by a camera placed in the hands of a native informant and those of the "objective" fieldworker has sometimes demonstrated. As John Collier, Jr., says in his excellent book. *Visual Anthropology: Photography as a Research Method*, "learning to observe visually, to see culture in all of its complex detail, can be a challenge to the fieldworker" [1967, p. 1]. He suggests, as we have throughout this book, that anyone planning fieldwork accept the "challenge of observation." Practice in being observant is, obviously, of great value in field photography. So practice giving a second look at things in your everyday world, concentrating even on tiny details. Think how you would treat them if you were looking through a camera's viewfinder. The art of seeing can play an important role in making photography more exciting for you and for those who enjoy your photographic work. One Kodak booklet suggests being a "head hunter" and learning to catch fleeting expressions.

With regard to how to begin photographing in the field and

158   ANTHROPOLOGY FIELD PROJECTS

where to start, Collier notes that we cannot assume that everyone wants his picture taken. In a few parts of the world, indeed, one may encounter religious rules against allowing oneself to be photographed at all. There may also be social constraints. In Mexico you can be arrested for photographing poverty [Collier 1967, p. 15]. In some parts of Europe it is illegal to photograph strangers without their permission. Obviously, from these few examples, it can be seen that societies vary greatly in what they consider to be subjects that are sensitive, or even so morally wrong or emotionally charged as to be outlawed altogether. Collier makes some suggestions that parallel others in this book, but which are worth quoting here because of their specific relevance for photography:

> Fieldworkers have found they can safely approach human organizations by operating in logical sequence, *from the public to the most private* [italics his], from the formal to the informal, in a reasonable fashion from the outside in. The rule of thumb might be: photograph first what the natives are most proud of! [p. 15].

As concerns photography, then, if the fieldworker is careful not to overstep the bounds of good judgment, it may be possible to start rapid and accurate collection of data on uncontroversial subjects even before he or she has acquired sufficiently extensive knowledge of many aspects of the cultural scene to make adequate verbal descriptions. Collier also suggests, as we have earlier, that the first phases of fieldwork usually include a variety of descriptive processes, including mapping and sketching, and suggests the use of photography in connection with those operations. Aerial photography can, of course, also provide an accurate base for creating maps and for showing the relationship of cultural features to each other, the presence or absence of natural resources, patterns of land use, and a wealth of other details about human relationship to social and physical environment. Getting down to earth, if the fieldworker does not have access to aerial photographs, a series of pictures taken from some high spot may prove to be an important aid in constructing a map. If the ethnographer is especially interested in the physical setting of his fieldwork, a few hours' walk with the camera might enable him to get a complete overview of the community under study — for example, the types of housing, markets and shops, transportation facilities, public buildings — the details of which would be impossible or extremely time-consuming for him to record by any other method.

With the passage of time and the establishment of trust, the ethnographer can begin to do more informal or more personal photographing of individuals and their lifeways. We have mentioned previously that, like most modern ethnographers, we prefer to work with informants who are not paid directly for their help, partly because we feel that, as a general rule, this improves the quality of the relationships that can be established. This in no way implies less sense of responsibility or indebtedness toward informants; but our "payments" over the years are now part of the whole complex that is friendship. One way in which we try to repay a portion of the hospitality and assistance given us is through the giving of photographs. One of us has consistently given every person a copy of each photograph in which he appears, with the exception of group photographs. Although somewhat expensive, photographs have proven to be eagerly welcomed gifts and also the means of preserving memories of occasions shared by the ethnographer and his or her informants. One recently widowed mother of twelve said, "That is the only picture of their father my children will ever have." The giving of photographs might also be a very good thing for you to consider doing in conjunction with some of your work with informants for this course.

As the fieldwork proceeds, the ethnographer can begin to use his growing collection of photographs as an aid in structuring interviews without the sometimes inhibiting effects of formal questionnaires or verbal probes that might seem to be tiring or unnecessary to the informant. A carefully presented sequence of pictures on a particular subject about which the fieldworker wants information will channel the interview more or less within the subject area of interest, and will often help the informant to remember relevant information that might otherwise have been forgotten. Instead of directly interrogating the informant, the fieldworker can join with him in examining photographs. Thus, the images become the object of discussion and the focus of attention, so the informant has a greater feeling of freedom than if he were being questioned directly. Photographs often call forth more than mere descriptions of what is represented, and can serve as a valuable means for getting at the deeper aspects of the culture—the feelings, attitudes, values, emotions, and so on.

The ways photographs can be used in gathering information—and, as a bonus, gaining additional degrees of rapport—may vary greatly according to circumstances. A friend of ours who conducted his research at a fishing beach and who did his own developing in the field, established the custom of displaying a new set of pictures each week on the wall of the shop where most of the men congregated to eat their meals and buy their soft drinks. The weekly display evoked a great deal of interest and useful comment. The presence of the photos served to introduce the newcomers who frequently arrived at the beach to the idea that they, too, might expect to have their pictures taken, and that those already on the beach were not only allowing themselves to be photographed but seemed to have a friendly relationship with the man taking the photographs. One aspect of this study should be thought about in conjunction with an important rule of thumb which Collier gives on the basis of his extensive experience: "Pictures taken in the public domain can be fed back into the public domain. Pictures made in private circumstances *should be shown only to people in these circumstances*" [p. 44].

For the anthropologist interested in recording technology, be he archaeologist or ethnographer, photography has long been recognized as an invaluable research method. The ethnographer may, for example, make a series of shots showing some technological process. By showing the photographs to the craftsman, he can then gain a better understanding of the tools, materials, and processes involved, including important steps that may have been slighted in the first photographs.

Photographs are also important in making inventories of material culture. In addition to tangible content that may be analyzed and/or counted, classified and correlated, the pictures may yield data on a less tangible level as well—on the effect or meaning that all the tangible content observed might have on the people, on the quality of life of the family, and on their methods of coping with the world around them.

One way in which the use of photographs has increased rapidly in the last thirty years is in the documentation of human interaction. The complexities of social events can be captured for future interpretation, comparison, and quantification. Collecting photographs to use as data on human interaction is sometimes especially rewarding when carried out in the form of "structured observations." This involves obtaining comparable images by photographing the particular type of social interaction under study as often as possible, under conditions that are as constant as possible. Margaret Mead and Gregory Bateson did pioneering studies of this type. (See particularly their *Balinese Character: A Photographic Analysis*, 1942.) For example, the series of comparison shots exploring how Balinese adults relate to children illustrates the inattentiveness of the hands of adults as they hold and nurse small children. Once comparable situations have been photographed, there are a number of levels at which the data in the photographs can be read. The first level involves the simple discovery, observation, and enumeration of individual variables as they appear in each picture. At this level one may, for example, be noting the number of people wearing shoes as opposed to those in sandals, the proportions of men, women, and children in groups assembled on various ceremonial occasions, or any phenomena that seem to warrant further study. On other levels of study, correlation of variables that appear together in photographs might be meaningful, or measurable and quantifiable differences in variables might be examined further.

The use of photography is essential in any extensive study of nonverbal communication as a form of social interaction. Body posture, facial expression, hand gestures, and spatial relationships are all rapidly and accurately recorded in photographs for use in studies of proxemics and kinesics. (Kinesics is the study of culturally patterned postures and gestures.) The camera can preserve all the wealth of detail that would be impossible to capture with notebook and pencil alone.

ABOUT PHOTOGRAPHIC EQUIPMENT AND ITS USE

We realize that students in a course such as this one will be likely to represent a great range of experience in photography, from the real beginner to the practiced near-professional. We realize, also, that many of you will be using borrowed equipment with which you are not familiar. We have, therefore, chosen to go into some detail on the technical aspects of photography in order that you may be able to refer to it from time to time when necessary while "on assignment" in the field.

As a first order of business, we would like to suggest that when you visit a camera shop to get film for your project you take the opportunity to look around at some of the available equipment and literature. As one who may be increasing your use of photographic equipment and supplies in the future, it is a good idea to begin to familiarize yourself with what a camera shop has to offer in supplies and in suggestions. If you are a beginner in photography, it might, in fact, be a very good idea to start by asking for some specialized advice about the film you are there to buy, for the best choice will depend not only on the camera you will use, but on several other factors as well.

There has been a marked increase during the last five or ten years in locally established or travelling teams representing various photographic supply houses. The nature and extent of the services that these groups provide varies somewhat, but you may find that one is available in your locality and a representative could come to your class to give a talk and consult with you, if you like.

One of the services that is available nationwide is that of the Audio-Visual Booking Desk at Eastman Kodak Company, Department 841, 343 State Street, Rochester, New York 14650 (or telephone area code 716, 325-2000, and ask for the Audio-Visual Booking Desk). From Kodak your class could obtain a small catalog of their many shows in movies and slides, which are loaned free of charge. The slide programs, for example, also include tape recordings for sound accompaniment, a script for the person who changes slides, and information leaflets for all who see the program to take home. Obviously, not all of the programs would be appropriate for application in anthropological fieldwork.

The material that follows gives a general overview of some of the basic concepts and terminology you will deal with in the use of your camera. The technical side of picture taking is basically simple enough that it should not take you long to learn. In any case, the objective is to learn to take pictures to suit your ethnographic purposes, not to get a job as a professional photographer. Study the instructions that come with your camera and the film you are using, since both were written by experts. The film instructions are written for both simple and complex cameras (also simple and complex photographers). The bibliography at the end of this project gives some references you can consult if you want to extend your knowledge. This discussion concentrates on the operation of still cameras, since they are simpler to use and cheaper to own and operate than most movie and videotape equipment. Even if you are oriented toward moving pictures, you will benefit from a solid grounding in the use of still equipment.

Essentially, a camera is nothing more than a light-tight box that holds the film and to which is attached the lens, which can project an image onto the film when the user wishes it to. Usually, a camera has controls attached to it that allow the user to aim the camera at the subject he wants to photograph, to focus the image onto the film, and to regulate the amount of light that reaches the film. Definitions of terms and their interrelationships are given below.

Beyond these minimal qualifications, the sky is almost literally the limit in terms of the elaboration and sophistication (and the cost!) of photographic equipment that is available or which can be created. It is easy to be dazzled by all of the gadgets that are available – or to find arguments proclaiming that only certain kinds of cameras should be considered at all – and to end up with something that is far too specialized, too costly, or otherwise unsuited to your needs.

Cameras can be classified on the bases of focusing system and size of film used. There are many combinations from which to choose. The cameras that are probably the most popular with anthropologists today are those with single- or twin-lens reflex focusing systems, which take 35 mm. and 120 or 220 film, respectively.

A fixed-focus camera usually has a viewfinder, which will give a fairly accurate idea of what the lens will take if the subject is distant (a landscape or building) or at middle distance (group shots and so forth), but becomes increasingly inaccurate the closer you approach the subject. Some can be used only in good light or with a flash; but more and more really inexpensive fixed-focus cameras now can be used in a variety of situations, especially with new high-speed (see below) film. Instructions accompanying these cameras generally tell how to use them under different conditions. On the whole, however, fixed-focus cameras are not flexible enough for many fieldwork uses.

Zone-focus cameras (where the user measures or guesses the distance to the subject and can set the lens to that distance) are intermediate between fixed-focus and rangefinder cameras. They are also generally inadequate for anthropological purposes.

Rangefinder (RF) cameras provide a linkage between the lens and the viewfinder so the user can tell not only what the lens is "looking at," but also when the image should be in focus on the film. Most commonly, two images of the subject are projected into the viewfinder, and the user turns the lens focusing mechanism until these two images overlap exactly, showing the image will be in focus on the film. Although generally easy to focus, RF cameras do not tell the user how much of the image on the film will be in focus (see depth of field discussion below), or whether the focusing linkage is working correctly. One problem with RF cameras is the "parallax error" that results from the difference in position of the viewfinder and the taking lens. This causes no real difficulty with distant scenes but becomes acute in close-ups. You can correct for parallax by tipping the camera slightly in the direction of the viewfinder after you have composed the picture. Some high-quality RF cameras have devices that provide some compensation for parallax.

Reflex cameras provide for the focusing to be done through the lens. Single-lens reflexes (SLR's) have the viewing, focusing, and taking all done through the same lens, so the user can tell quite accurately what will be in the picture, and parallax error is eliminated. A prism, which is part of this focusing system, gives most SLR's their characteristic bump in the top middle part of the body; and this prism, along with a mirror that moves during exposure, makes most SLR's bigger, more complicated mechanically, and more expensive than RF cameras. The mirror movement also makes noise during exposure, a feature that sometimes makes unobstrusive use of the camera difficult. With a few cameras, such as the noisy Besselar Topcon, for example, it is almost impossible to take a second shot that is "candid."

Twin-lens reflex (TLR) cameras have two lenses connected together, usually one above the other. The image from one lens is reflected onto ground glass (ground so as to be "frosted" and hence make the image easy to see), so that the user can tell what the lens is seeing and when the subject image is in focus, while the image from the other lens is projected onto the film when the shutter is opened. Thus, although the TLR is mechanically more rugged and simpler than either the RF or SLR cameras, it is also subject to parallax error, since the viewing lens is seeing a slightly different image than the taking lens. These cameras are generally much bulkier than either the RF or SLR cameras.

"View" cameras, which usually look like accordions, are the cameras with which ground-glass focusing is most commonly associated. The lens is attached to the front of the camera body, and the position of the front is moved back and forth (and sometimes up and down) until the image is in focus on the ground glass at the back. This image, although upside down and reversed, can be studied to see what will be in the final picture and what the depth of field will be. Before the exposure can be made, a sheet of film is placed where the ground glass was. View cameras generally take large film sizes, and hence are bulky, as well as slow, to use. They are seldom useful for general-purpose fieldwork, although they may be good choices for detailed pictures at one locus, such as at an archaeological dig.

Film can be classified in different ways. The kind of camera you have determines the size and types of films you can use.

The smallest commonly available roll film is about 16 mm. in width, or approximately the same width as 110 size film, which comes only in special "drop in" cartridges. The major drawback to these film sizes is that the small negatives they give (and hence any dust, dirt or defects in or on them) must be enlarged many times to reach normal print sizes. In addition, the cartridges are inherently wasteful because they cannot be reloaded, nor can cameras made for them be used with any other film types. (Note that 110, 126, 120, and 220 are manufacturers' designations for particular film sizes, though the numbers have no necessary connection to the physical size of the film.)

Drop-in loading cartridges in the 126 size have some of the same disadvantages as the 110 size; but the negatives are usually 28 mm. square and do require less enlarging to cover normal print sizes.

One of the most widely used film sizes is 135, which is 35 mm. wide. The film is usually packed in standardized cassettes, some of which can be reloaded with film by the user, who can then buy film in long rolls and make considerable savings in film costs by "rolling his own." The standard 35 mm. negative size is 24×36 mm., though some "half frame" cameras that use this film make negatives only 18×24 mm. Since money can be saved by reloading cassettes, and since it is possible to get up to 36 exposures per roll on film which yields negatives of a fairly useful size, 35 mm. film is relatively economical. The advantage of being able to take 36 exposures without reloading can be appreciated readily by anyone who has ever been cheated of wonderful opportunities for photographs by running out of film at a crucial moment. Another advantage is that this is a widely available size.

Film in the 120 and 220 sizes is slightly over $2\frac{1}{2}$ inches in width, with 220 roles longer than 120. These sizes give $2\frac{1}{4} \times 2\frac{1}{4}$-inch ($6 \times 6$ cm.) or $2\frac{1}{4} \times 2\frac{3}{4}$-inch ($6 \times 7$ cm.) negatives. Generally speaking, since larger negatives yield better-quality photographs, this size of film is inherently capable of higher quality than 35 mm.

Most Polaroid films come in rolls. They generally do not give negatives in the sense used here, but rather give completed prints developed immediately after the exposure; there is more discussion of Polaroid below.

The choice of a general-purpose camera usually involves a compromise between the physical size of the camera (the smaller and lighter, the easier to carry) and the film size (the larger the negative, the better the quality of the pictures). For most anthropological purposes, cameras giving 24×36 mm. negatives on 35 mm. film, or $2\frac{1}{4}$-inch-square or larger negatives on 120 or 220 film represent the best compromise. The discussion above gives an idea of some of the other options available. You should think through your requirements carefully before you get a camera for your use, since "what everybody else is using" may not be suitable for you.

Lenses are generally thought of in terms of their focal lengths and their maximum apertures or "speeds." The focal length indicates the approximate length of the lens in terms of the optics involved, and is important because the longer the focal length the greater the magnification of any image on the film. (Lenses with great focal length are often called telephoto lenses.) Conversely, the shorter the focal length, the larger is the field of view, and hence the number of subjects (as with so-called wide-angle lenses). Most cameras come with lenses that are called normal, or standard, focal lengths, which means that the lens will put onto the film approximately the field of view seen by the human eye. Some cameras have their lenses permanently fixed to the body, while others take lenses that can be detached and interchanged with those of other focal lengths.

Since lenses are designed to admit light, an important feature of a lens is the amount of light it can transmit to the film. Generally speaking, the more light a lens can transmit, the "faster" it is said to be or the greater "speed" it has. At the same time, in order to ensure that exactly the right amount of light gets to the film, some way is needed to cut down the amount of light transmitted. This regulation is done by an iris diaphragm, which works on the same principle as the human eye, whereby the diaphragm is closed down (or "stopped down") so that the hole, or aperture, through it is made smaller in order to cut down the amount of light going through. Lenses are calibrated in f-stops that indicate relatively how much light they let through. The f-stops form a standard sequence (1, 1.4, 2, 2.8, 4, 5.6, 8, 11, 16, etc.), with each larger number indicating that the diaphragm hole has been made enough smaller to cut in half the amount of light going through.

Now that we have talked about camera types and lenses, we can consider the three basic camera controls, of which the first, focusing, has already been covered. The other two, aperture setting and shutter speed, are directly related to giving the correct exposure or amount of light to the film, and their operation is interrelated. In addition to controlling light transmission, as discussed above, the aperture setting controls the depth of field. This simply means the distance range in front of and behind the principal subject in which the objects in the pictures are in sharp focus. Although you usually focus on one subject, you are interested in knowing how many other objects in front of and behind that principal subject will also be in focus in the final picture. In terms of the lens, the smaller the aperture (the higher the f-stop number), the greater will be the depth of field. You must, therefore, set the aperture so as to include in the depth of field all the objects you want to record clearly. If you want to emphasize some object over others, one way is to have a shallow depth of field that covers only the principal object and leaves the others blurred.

The shutter speed is a statement of how long light is admitted to the film; this time is usually expressed in fractions of a second. The usual progression is: 1, $\frac{1}{2}$, $\frac{1}{4}$, $\frac{1}{8}$, $\frac{1}{15}$, $\frac{1}{30}$, $\frac{1}{60}$, $\frac{1}{125}$, $\frac{1}{250}$, $\frac{1}{500}$, $\frac{1}{1000}$, although other speeds are, of course, possible, and some cameras do not go as high as $\frac{1}{1000}$th second. (Note that these are often written on the camera as whole numbers — 1, 2, 4, 8, 60, 500, etc. — since it is understood that they are fractions.) Each speed is double the next slower one, and one-half the next higher, so that this progression is complementary to the f-stop progression. Beyond regulating the light, the shutter speed is important in preventing blurred pictures. An overall blur of everything in the exposure can come about if the shutter speed is slow and the camera is moved during the exposure. If you have difficulties with such overall blurring of pictures, try leaning on something stable; resting the camera on a wall, a chairback, or a table; increasing the firmness of your control of the camera by holding one or both elbows tightly against the body; or, as one of us has, form a life-long habit of holding your breath when you snap the shutter! The blurring of a moving subject can come about when the subject is moving fast enough so it moves while the shutter is open; the faster the shutter speed (the less time it is open), the faster the motion that can be "frozen" by the camera. As one Kodak "Here's How" booklet suggests, capturing speed is best done with speed — a speedy film (see below), a fast shutter speed, speedy reflexes, and panning. Panning is the technique of following the motion of the subject with the camera. Panning will result in sharp reproduction of the subject you are following while blurring the background.

Shutter speed and aperture together determine the amount of light that reaches the film. For example, if you have determined that f5.6 at $\frac{1}{125}$ second is the correct exposure for the scene you want to photograph, and yet you want to get more depth of field by stopping down one f-stop to f8, you must then slow the shutter speed down one setting, to $\frac{1}{60}$. Thus f4 at $\frac{1}{250}$, and f5.6 at $\frac{1}{125}$, and f8 at $\frac{1}{60}$, etc., are equivalent exposures in the sense that they all put the same amount of light onto the film, but are not equivalent in terms of their implications for depth of field or ability to stop action. You need to decide which combination of exposure settings is best for your purposes.

Film, which we have already discussed in terms of size, is basically a light-sensitive chemical emulsion coated on some kind of clear backing that is physically strong enough to take handling. It must always be kept in complete darkness until exposed within the camera to the correct amount of light. After exposure, it is processed in various chemicals that "develop" the image so that it can be seen with the eye, and then "fixed" so that the image will not fade away.

Films can be classified, in addition to physical size, on the basis of how they reproduce colors. Black-and-white films reproduce colors as shades of gray, while color films approximate the colors of the original subject. In addition, films can be classified on the basis of degree of sensitivity to light. Fast films require relatively less light to make an image, and hence are more useful for picture taking under dim light conditions, while slow films require a lot of light for acceptable exposure. Film sensitivity is given a numerical rating, called ASA ratings in the United States and DIN ratings in Europe. The two sets of ratings are equivalent, although the numbers are different. In general, the faster the film, the "grainier" it looks and the less its ability to record fine detail, so there is little to be gained from using film that is faster than necessary for the light conditions under which it is to be used.

With negative films, the film image is the reverse of the original scene—where the scene was bright, the negative is dark, and where the scene was dark, the film was less exposed and hence is light, or may even have no noticeable image at all. Negatives are usually intermediate steps in the production of the final image, for light is projected through the negative onto light-sensitive paper (a photographic emulsion coated on a paper base instead of a film base) so that the result (the negative of a negative) comes out a positive in the final "projection print," usually just called a "print."

With most Polaroid films, there is no negative but only a finished print or transparency, and copies can be made only by photographing the print, thus Polaroid is intermediate between negative films and reversal films, which are discussed below. The lack of a negative (and, hence, of easy reproducibility), the high cost per picture, and the bulkiness of the cameras make Polaroid equipment relatively unsuited for general-purpose anthropological photography, although some people like to use them in addition to other cameras because the prints can be given to picture subjects immediately.

With reversal films, the piece of film that was exposed in the camera is processed to come out as a positive. That is, it can be viewed directly without the need for further manipulation (although the resulting transparency—so called because it is transparent to light—is often projected for easier viewing, especially if it is of small size, as is the case with 35 mm. slides). Color reversal film, by and large, has less tolerance for exposure errors (less "latitude") than negative films, and, if prints are desired, a negative must be made by special techniques. As with the Polaroid print, if the original is lost or damaged, there is no way to get another without retaking the picture.

The fact that prints and transparencies have to be displayed in different ways should be kept in mind when film choices are made. To some extent, transparencies can be made into prints, and negatives used to make transparencies, although this may raise the cost and diminish the quality of the final product. A useful way to catalog negatives is to place them directly on a sheet of photographic paper and expose the paper to light to make a contact print, which can then be studied without damaging the negatives by handling and without the expense of enlarging every negative. After the sheet has been studied, the best or most useful negatives can be chosen for enlargement, and the contact sheet kept as a record of that roll of film.

Many of the operations mentioned above in relation to developing film, making prints, and so forth, can be done by those who have access to a photographic darkroom. It would be instructive for you to practice with developing and printing if you get a chance, since it deepens your grasp of how photography works. However, for the purpose of the assignments to be given below, it will not be necessary for you to do your own darkroom work.

Light meters, or exposure meters, are devices used to measure the amount of light coming from or going to the subject. Most of these meters transfer the light reading to a set of dials that indicate the range of f-stops and shutter speeds that will give correct exposure. Light meters can be mounted inside a camera, or outside it, or held in the hand. If the light meters are inside, as they are on some cameras, they are connected to the exposure controls so that the camera can make correct exposures automatically. One must be sure to take the meter reading from the principal subject. If, for instance, you want to take a picture of someone standing in shadow but with bright sunlight behind, most meters (those which are "averaging" meters) give a reading based on the whole scene and would indicate an exposure that would result in your principal subject's being badly underexposed. It is better to over- or underexpose the less important portions of a picture and concentrate on giving the best treatment for the thing you want most to capture. In the absence of a meter, the literature that comes with the film usually has the manufacturer's suggested exposures for different common lighting situations.

In terms of your assignments and later use of photography, the most important thing about your photographic equipment is that you know how to use it. This comes about through practice and thoughtful study of the results of your picture taking. *Never* take untried and untested equipment into the field or on a major assignment. As we have discussed here, you do not need to spend a lot of money on a camera. What you do want is equipment that is suited to your needs and flexible enough to be adapted to your requirements. If you do not have a suitable camera at present, consider buying good used equipment rather than cheap new equipment. Remember not to be dazzled into buying something unless its technical features will be useful to you. It is also often possible to borrow or rent supplementary equipment.

Although it is important to know, and to know how to use, the capacities of a more flexible camera, other factors are of great importance in the final results. An otherwise excellent photo may, for instance, suffer from poor composition. You may be concentrating on the principal subject and not be aware of other things in the picture that the camera will faithfully record, such as background trees appearing to grow out of the subject's head. A distant figure may seem clear to you but turn out as a small blot in the final picture. In general, good composition calls for a balanced picture, with attention being drawn to a strong center of interest. If that main center of interest is smack in the middle of the picture, it tends to look static and uninteresting; so does a picture that the horizon exactly bisects. Lines should lead into, not out of, the picture, guiding the eye to the main subject. The rectangular format of a 35 mm. camera is a useful aid in arriving at pleasing composition. Use the long axis for strongly vertical subjects by turning the camera sideways. The background can make or break a picture. It can help to set the mood; but it can also distract badly if it is cluttered. In good weather, try shooting from a low angle to include sky. In scenic shots, it is often a good idea to include people in the foreground—but people who are looking at the scene, not woodenly at the camera. A final hint concerning composition that is often given—and often needed—is to move in close to your subject until you have eliminated everything that does not add to your picture. Some people look through the viewfinder and start backing away. This is neither the best way to compose, nor the best way to survive to take more pictures.

When shooting color film, it is generally a good idea to try to include variation in color; with black and white, try for contrast. But neither of these suggestions, nor any of those about composition above, is to be taken as a rule. You may, for instance, want to portray the total greenness of a rainforest, or the total grayness of a foggy winter morning. A camera is only as good as the photographer behind it. But some people, who have little technical expertise, have an excellent feel for attaining good composition, for seizing precisely the right moments to catch people being themselves, and for generally capturing the spirit of a people and their ways of life on film. Such people can succeed very well as ethnographic photographers.

THE PROJECT

This project consists of nine photographs. While only one photograph of each of nine types is required, those of you who would like to experiment more with the use of your equipment may wish to make several exposures of some types that you can analyze for what they can tell you about your camera and its use under various conditions. If you shoot color transparencies, make sure there will be some way to project them for comparison with others in class—or you may want to have prints made from the transparencies. As you put together the nine photos for the project, ask yourself to what extent each could stand on its own without a caption.

For the purposes of this project (and, of course, for what you can learn from the information), please keep a record for each exposure of when it was made, the equipment (camera and lens, if you have a choice of more than one of either), shutter speed, f-stop, the film and the exposure index for it, and, if possible, the light-meter readings taken. With experience, you may not need to keep all of these records; but they are invaluable at first. Dating is the one type of record that must never be omitted.

1. *A street scene.* Select a street scene on a sunny day that gives deep shadows, as well as very bright areas. If you have a light meter, take readings in both the shadows and the highlights. Decide on a compromise exposure setting that is somewhere between the settings you would make for the shadow and the highlight area. Please be sure not to have too shallow a depth of field for this picture, so that you can convey the feeling and action of a large enough area—perhaps most of a block. Examine your results, especially to see to what extent the compromise exposure gives both highlight and shadow detail. Use your best compromise exposure (if you have more than one) for the project.

2. *A building.* View a building that interests you at several times of day (photographing, of course, if you like), observing from the same position, preferably north or south of the building. Note the effect of light in modeling the building and emphasizing its three-dimensional nature. Tilt your camera up, and note that the building's walls appear to be converging. Choose the exposure that best shows the building's three-dimensional character.

3 and 4. *Artifacts.* Take separate exposures of a small artifact (man-made object) sized 3 inches or less, and of a larger artifact between 6 inches and 6 feet in size. Try exploring different angles for viewing the artifacts and different lighting arrangements. You will need at least one strong light to bring out the form and texture of the artifacts, as well as other (perhaps less strong) lights to keep the shadows from being underexposed and hence too dark for the film to record detail. Note that at close focusing distances your camera's lens has very little depth of field and you will need to stop it down as far as possible to get the artifacts in focus. You may need a tripod and cable release to help you because of the slow shutter speed, and may want to check on possible parallax error. If you have trouble in gauging distance from your lens, and, especially if the camera you are using requires you to "guesstimate," since exact focusing becomes especially necessary in close-ups, you may want to tie a string at the front of your camera near the lens. If you put a knot in the string at a distance from the camera that corresponds to the distance setting you use for the photograph, hold the string out from the camera until it touches the artifact and the string is taut. You can then drop the string and take photos at the desired distance. Use the two pictures that best show the artifacts for these parts of the project.

5 and 6. *Portraits.* Next take one portrait of a child and one of an adult, preferably taken so as to emphasize not only the face of the person but also the context within which he or she lives, works, or plays—the playroom or play area for the child, the home or office for the adult. Again,

you will want to experiment with lighting, either natural light or artificial light, or both. Part of the challenge will consist of putting the subject at ease so the pictures will be natural. Often this can be accomplished, at least in part, by giving him something to do. In working with a child, it is often a good idea to phrase your purpose in terms of wanting to photograph a doll or some other toy, so that the child just thinks of himself as helping to get the toy's picture. Perhaps you might arrange a "birthday party" for a doll or bear and invite the child to take part. Compose the portraits carefully enough to leave out objects and lights that would distract from the purpose of the picture. Remember that the camera is literal and records what you point it at, unlike the human eye, which can ignore what it does not want to see. Use the best pictures of the two people for these parts of the project.

7. *Small group interaction.* Select an outdoor group activity, and make your photograph one that attempts to capture interaction, as well as the context in which the people are acting (that is, the buildings, artifacts, and so forth, that give additional clues to the nature of the group and what they are doing). You want the practice of capturing human interaction in a still picture, which means that you need to compose the picture with enough depth of field and a fast enough shutter speed, as well as at a peak moment in the interaction. Select the exposure that best shows context and interaction, so that the resulting picture shows what the group of people is doing collectively, in contrast to a set of unrelated actions, and use it for the assignment.

8. *Stop action.* Choose a lively activity, such as a sporting event with lots of quick action, and photograph the action in accordance with our earlier suggestions—use a fast shutter speed and pan with the action to "freeze" the principal subject. Concentrate on catching a peak action moment. Use your best action-stopping exposure for the project.

9. *An interior.* Photograph the inside of a room to show the furniture and other artifacts, and their arrangement. Such photographs are often used by anthropologists for general illustrative purposes, as well as part of inventories of material culture. If you have any supplementary equipment, such as a tripod, a cable release, additional lighting devices or flash, you may wish to use them for this assignment, although the use of available light is, of course, permissible. Correct camera settings for use with flash can be determined with the aid of the instruction sheet provided with each roll of film. Select an angle of view that shows the room and its contents clearly, and a depth of field to cover everything you want in the final picture. If you use flash, aim at an angle to any reflecting surface so as not to have a reflected ball of light in your picture. Flash may be useful

to you for a picture such as this, whereas it often is not when photographing people or public events, because it draws so much attention to the photographer and makes activity less spontaneous. Choose your best exposure for this part of the project.

SELECTED ANNOTATED BIBLIOGRAPHY

Bateson, Gregory, and Margaret Mead
    Balinese Character: A Photographic Analysis. The New York Academy of Sciences. Special Publications of the New York Academy of Sciences, Vol. II, 1942. A classic example of the use of photography in culture and personality studies. One of the few published examples of the consistent application of photography as a primary means of gathering data.

Byers, Paul
    "Still Photography in Systematic Recording and Analysis of Behavioral Data." *Human Organization,* 1964, 23:78–84. Contains a good discussion of the difference between what the camera "sees" and what the human eye "sees." It emphasizes using the camera as a means of recording significant aspects of social interaction, rather than just taking pictures for illustration purposes.

Collier, John, Jr.
    Visual Anthropology: Photography as a Research Method. Holt, Rinehart and Winston, 1967. This book is the basic reference for the student interested in using photography in fieldwork. It contains a complete discussion of the uses of photography in fieldwork, including the planning and executing of research that uses photography as a primary source of data.

Feininger, Andreas
    Basic Color Photography. Amphoto, 1972. A clear and concise guide to the selection and use of camera and film, applicable to black-and-white, as well as color, photography.

Mead, Margaret, and Ken Heyman
    Family. Macmillan, 1965. An anthropologist and photographer combine to create an amply illustrated book about the family in cross-cultural perspective.

Rudisill, Richard
    Mirror Image. University of New Mexico Press, 1971. A story of the early beginnings of photography.

Steichen, Edward, comp.
    The Family of Man. New York Museum of Modern Art, 1955. The great photographic collection of 503 photos from 68 countries.

Worth, Sol, and John Adair
    "Navajo Filmmakers." *American Anthropologist,* 1970, 72(1): 9–34. A report on some of the first innovative experiments in which members of the society being investigated were asked to make films, choosing their own subject matter.

* * *

Directories and buying guides to photographic equipment are usually put out once a year or so by the editors of photographic magazines, such as *Modern Photography* and *Popular Photography*, and are useful summaries of the kinds of equipment available. Current issues of photographic magazines often have articles on different aspects of photography suitable for beginners and advanced amateurs.

Eastman Kodak Company, Rochester, New York, 14650. Kodak supplies information on how to use its camera and film products as well as Data Books, "Here's How" Books, and other publications on numerous aspects of photography. Most photographic dealers carry many of these publications and can get others for you, from this and other companies. Many Kodak booklets are less than one dollar; and there is a special packet of eighty items for the amateur at three dollars.

Editors of Time-Life Books have a series in the Life Library of Photography, including ones on the camera, light and film, the print, color, etc. These books include information on the history of photography, as well as current practices, are lavishly illustrated with diagrams and photographs, and are reasonably priced.

Society for the Anthropology of Visual Communication (formerly Program in Ethnographic Film). The newsletters of this organization are a valuable source of information about the current opinions as to how films may be used in anthropology. Also included are reviews and discussions of the ethnographic films which are currently being produced.

PROJECT FOURTEEN

PLANNING A COMMUNITY STUDY

INTRODUCTION

Throughout this book, we have often used the word "community," both in the introductory sections dealing with the theoretical foundations of particular research methods and in the instructions for the projects themselves. In general, we have used "community" loosely to refer to whatever group was chosen as the focus for your projects (for example, the church congregation of the participant observation chapter, the ethnic group from whom your examples of folklore were collected, and so forth). For the purposes of most of those chapters, then, we have used the term in a fairly flexible manner, applying it to very different types of human groupings, both formal and informal, cohesive and dispersed.

However, a very important branch of field anthropology has been devoted to a more precise definition of the concept of community, and to the use of the community as the basis of ethnographic research. Because this "community study school" has been so influential in contemporary anthropology, and because it has attempted to bring together into a unified framework so many of the approaches discussed in this book, we feel it appropriate to round off our survey of ways of collecting data in the field with a discussion of the community.

According to one dictionary, a community may be defined as "a body of people having common organizations or interests, or living in the same place under the same laws and regulations." As such, social scientists have always studied "communities" insofar as they were interested in human groups. The terms "society" and "culture" were developed in order to discuss these groups on a higher level of abstraction; but what people actually worked with were communities, the collections of people whom one could observe, live among, and describe. A more formal usage of the community concept developed early in this century, primarily among sociologists interested in studying the city in particular as a "natural laboratory of social science" [Hollingshead 1948, p. 136]. At that time, the city was defined in terms of its *norms*, and sociologists were frequently interested in improving the lot of those unfortunates who, for one reason or another, were unable to live up to those standards [Hollingshead, p. 137]. In this rather restricted use of the concept of community, the unit focused upon was not simply everybody living in the same place at the same time, but only those who conformed to certain patterns of approved behavior.

In the 1920s a group of sociologists at the University of Chicago turned away from this normative (and interventionist) approach to the community. They saw the city not as a natural laboratory in which they could practice social engineering but as a unit of *analysis*. According to the members of the "Chicago School," the role of the social scientist was to study particular communities in terms of their history, development, population, and organization. The goal, then, was not to work to see that everyone conformed to "normal" standards, but to observe and account for variation as it naturally existed [Hollingshead, p. 137].

The most frequently cited achievement of this group was the study of "Middletown" by Robert and Helen Lynd, published in 1929. This was the first truly analytical study of a "typical" American town; and, although the Lynds were trained as sociologists, they made use of some of the basic techniques of the early ethnographers. They studied the ordinary, day-to-day lives of the people with whom they lived on a protracted basis, and, from that "inside" view, they were able to analyze the institutions, organizations, and other aspects of the social structure of the town. The Middletown project thus brought the notion of "interaction" into the vocabulary of community study. The point was not to define standards and then try to fit everyone into them, but to see who actually did what, with what, to whom, and with whom. The community, then, need not be localized. As long as people interacted in a regular way with each other, there might be said to be a community structure—even if they communicated only by mail or telephone.

One of the most prominent anthropologists at the University of Chicago at that time was Robert Redfield, who was very much influenced by the sociological group. As a result, he was able to combine his training in ethnography with the concerns of the community-oriented sociologists. Redfield is sometimes credited with ending anthropology's almost exclusive preoccupation with primitive tribal groups, and with introducing anthropological insights in the study of more complex societies, via the organizing principle of the community study.

Redfield's definitions of community are no longer fully accepted by anthropologists, but they are of sufficient importance to be discussed in some detail here. Redfield was concerned with what he termed the "little community," which he felt was the most characteristic form of human settlement throughout history, and even in the contemporary world [1955, p. 4]. When a researcher first enters any community, he will see only a mass of confusing activity—a totality that almost engulfs him because he cannot yet comprehend it. Using the ethnographic approach (as well as that favored by the Chicago School), the researcher begins to study the parts that make up this whole, and then he proceeds to discern how the parts fit together. When he finishes his analysis, he is once again able to see the totality, but this time it makes sense to him because he knows how it is constructed. The "little community," for Redfield, is the basic unit of observation for analyzing how people put themselves and their productions into some sort of meaningful order [p. 22].

Redfield [p. 4] defined the "little community" in terms of four major dimensions:

- distinctiveness (the group itself must be conscious of the fact that it is a group; outsiders must also recognize that the group is a group)
- size (the group must be small enough to allow members to interact with each other on an ongoing basis)
- homogeneity (members of the group must share a set of institutions, attitudes, values, etc.)
- self-sufficiency (the group must not be dependent on another group, for such dependence would affect the distinctive character of its own institutions)

Clearly, these criteria are based on a model of the community borrowed from the traditional anthropological research into tribal societies, and it has struck some critics as unfortunate that Redfield chose to treat the community in a more complex society—one which almost never is as completely self-sufficient as, say, a hunting/gathering group—as if it were a totally separate unit. In fairness to Redfield, it should be pointed out that he did not view the "little community," wherever in the world it happened to be, as if it were a totally detached entity, complete unto itself. Rather, such communities were seen as part of a continuum of complexity that ranged from the "folk" society up to the "urban" complex. While it is impossible to set precise boundaries and say that one thing is a "pure" folk community, for example, it is certainly clear that some communities more nearly approach one end of the spectrum than another in terms of their organizations and institutions. Since its contacts with the "great tradition" surrounding it will be minimal, a group that is relatively more "folk" can, then, be treated as if it were a self-sufficient unit—but *for purposes of analysis only.* Using such a definition, Redfield was able to study the Mayan village of Chan Kom in Mexico as a social entity whose institutions, activities, values, and so on could be analyzed in the same way as those of an isolated tribe, even though it had a marginal relationship to the sophisticated, literate cultural tradition of Hispanic America.

Redfield's work stimulated an interest in "peasant" studies—analyses of traditional (or "folk") communities within the urban civilizations of North and South America, Europe, and Asia. Although it is not necessary to survey this vast literature for the purposes of this chapter, at least one group of studies should be singled out because of the importance of the theory of community study that grew out of them. These are the studies of rural Irish life by Arensberg and Kimball [Arensberg 1937; Arensberg & Kimball 1940]. For various reasons, Arensberg and Kimball were unable to view the Irish village as a completely self-contained unit, as Redfield had done with Chan Kom; but they nevertheless recognized the importance of community as an organizational feature in all types of societies—the more complex and urban ones as well as the "folk" type.

In the 1950s and 1960s, Arensberg and Kimball were concerned with defining the notion of the community for analytical purposes, and with setting forth certain principles for studying a community in the field. Their first and most basic premise is that a community is not a "thing"—it is a *process* [Arensberg & Kimball 1965, p. 1]. It is, therefore, incorrect to ask, "What *is* a community?" Rather, one should ask, "What does a community *do*?" As a result, the researcher is advised to ". . . seek those regularities in the relationships among individuals that are revealed in their activities with each other and with the physical items in their environment" [1965, p. 2]. Whereas the social psychologist, for example, would study such regularities of interaction by setting up a controlled experimental group in a laboratory setting, the anthropologist (or sociologist) can use the community as a "living laboratory" – not as a field for working out social welfare plans, but as a setting for the formulation and testing of hypotheses [Arensberg 1961, p. 245].

What, then, in the view of Arensberg and Kimball, does the community do that makes it appropriate for the testing of hypotheses about society and culture in general? First and foremost, "Communities seem to be basic units of organization and transmission within a society and its culture" [Arensberg 1961, p. 248]. Thus, once again we have the criterion of a community being defined in terms of notions of communication and interaction, but with one important difference. It is not enough simply to communicate any old thing – one must communicate "culture." To refer to a somewhat more psychological frame of reference (which Arensberg and Kimball do not explicitly do), the community is the agency of socialization and enculturation, the vehicle by which children or newcomers are taught their statuses and roles as members of a sociocultural system. (See the discussion in Project 12.) In this way, Redfield's criterion of self-sufficiency can be retained; although the community may be in almost constant contact with communities elsewhere, to trade goods and services, perhaps, each community may very well retain its own autonomy as long as it retains its most basic institutions. (Depending on the particular group, these may include the family, the legal system, religious organizations, and the like.) A collection of such interconnected but autonomous communities may, indeed, form a cohesive "society" [Arensberg & Kimball 1965, p. 5], and much discussion has taken place over the nature of "plural" societies, whose units have different basic institutions, particularly in the Caribbean, East Africa, and South Asia.

Because the community, wherever it is and whatever its particular features may be, is a unit for the transmission of culture, it may be studied not only as a thing of interest in and of itself (as Redfield studied Chan Kom), but as a microcosm of the sociocultural system in which it is embedded [Arensberg 1955, p. 1143]. The true nature of the community study, then, is *naturalistic* (that is, observing the group as it is, rather than as a part of an experimental design), and *comparative* (studying communities as representatives of cultures that can be compared with one another, rather than as independent units studied as separate "things") [Arensberg & Kimball 1965, p. 29].

One studies a community, then, in much the same way that one studies a tribal society in classic ethnography: in totality. Although one may enter the field with a specific hypothesis to test, or a particular area of culture in which one is most interested (religious behavior, political systems, or whatever), it is always necessary to do as complete a study as possible of the community, in order to be able to understand the contexts in which the more specific behaviors occur. Obviously, it is impossible to study everything; but the goal of the community study is not "exhaustion in detail," but "depth in view" [Arensberg & Kimball 1965, p. 32]. This is achieved by what Arensberg and Kimball call a "multifactorial" approach [p. 31]; that is, one does not use just one of the research tools that have been outlined in this book—one uses all of them, if at all possible, and perhaps invents new ones that seem especially appropriate in the particular community being studied. The depth interview, participant observation, genealogical survey, life history collection, analysis of personal documents and of folklore, and all the rest are part of the complete community study [p. 31], not because they could ever possibly record every last fact and figure about the place, but because they shed light on so many different facets of the same behaviors.

The study of an American town by Barker and his associates [1968] is a conspicuous example of a community study in which "exhaustion in detail" was, in fact, chosen over "depth of view." This research team used a systematic method of observing and coding behaviors, specifically interpersonal interactions, making thousands of minute notations of everything that happened in specific localities. Barker, however, is a psychologist primarily interested in patterns of interaction, and not an anthropologist interested in sociocultural contexts of a broader type. While Barker's method is interesting and deserving of attention by anthropologists embarking on a community study, it should be noted that his study would not represent a "complete" community study as Arensberg and Kimball have defined the term.

One of the most important modifications within anthropology of the Arensberg and Kimball approach is that pioneered by Julian Steward. He rejects the premise that a community can be studied as if it were fully representative of a wider social system. He feels that in order to understand that sociocultural system it is necessary to study all of the different types of communities which make it up, as no one of them is likely to be fully representative. Obviously, this is an even more complex job than the "complete" study of just one community, and so Steward favors the use of a large research team, preferably one representing various other social sciences as well as anthropology. Smaller groups within this main research team would each be responsible for studying in depth one of several selected communities. The most important thing about doing research in this way is to insure *comparability* – to make sure that everyone is asking the same questions, in the same ways, observing the same types of things, and so on [Steward 1950, p. 25]. Each community must be studied and compared in terms of: its *local units* (households, streets, neighborhoods), its *special groups* (racial, caste, class, ethnic groups) and its *formal institutions* (political parties, church groups, service clubs, etc.) [Steward 1950, p. 115].

The most impressive example of Steward's approach to the community study is the massive Puerto Rico project [1956] he directed. The aim of this project was to study the social anthropology of Puerto Rico. Although the island is a distinct society with characteristic forms that make it different from other societies within the broad Hispanic-American tradition, there are many varieties within it. What are the roots of these variations within Puerto Rican society, and how are the various communities integrated into the whole of the Puerto Rican sociocultural system? In Steward's theory, the different types of Puerto Rican communities were based in large part on ecological adaptations; that is, communities in the mountains would clearly be different from those on the seacoast, from the point of view of adapting and obtaining a subsistence, and this difference would affect their respective social structures as well. Despite these ecological variations, however, all would bear the distinctive Puerto Rican stamp, marking them all as members of the same overall society. Therefore, a number of different communities, representative of the various types of ecological adaptation found on the island, were selected, and each was studied ethnographically, using research methods that had been standardized for use by all members of the research team. They all relied on:

- interviews, both random and directed
- collections of case histories
- participant observation
- key informant interviewing (interviewing specialists)

- use of archives, records, and other written documents, both historical and contemporary
- standardized questionnaires [see also Steward 1950, Chap. IV, for a summary of these procedures]

In a more narrowly bounded study, Raymond T. Smith analyzed three communities in British Guiana (now Guyana) in order to compare varieties in kinship and domestic organization [1956]. Smith's problem was that although there is something that might vaguely be termed a "West Indian kinship structure," and while there may well be a typically Guianese version thereof, it is useless to speak in such generalized terms when the variations actually reach down to the local community level. By selecting three communities that had different economic subsistence bases, and by studying the domestic arrangements in these groups, he was able to get a somewhat clearer view of what Guianese kinship really comprises. A roughly similar study was undertaken by Edith Clarke in Jamaica [1957].

THE PROJECT

Although you will probably not have the time or the resources to carry out a full-scale community study, you are now in a position, after having carried out some of the projects in this book, to make some tentative plans for such an undertaking.

Your project, then, is to write a proposal for a community study of your own home town or neighborhood, or any other full community with which you are very familiar. You may write it either as if you were planning to do it yourself, or as if you were answering a series of questions from another anthropologist who wanted to do it and was seeking your advice as an expert on this community.

Remember that a community is any *group* based on regular associations among persons; but this may be either a compact settlement with well-defined boundaries or a dispersed group whose boundaries overlap with the boundaries of other communities [M.G. Smith 1965, p. 176]. Pilcher's study of longshoremen in the city of Portland [1972] is an example of the latter. Although the people in question do not live in a spatially defined community (they live in various parts of town), they form a community because they share various important interactions, values, and attitudes with each other which they share with no other group in the city.

You may refer to the rather extensive outline prepared by Arensberg and Kimball [1965, pp. 36–40] that details the means of collecting data in a full-scale community study, or you may restrict yourself to the following more general outline.

I. Delimiting the community for study
    A. What are the boundaries of this community?
        1. Geographic boundaries (e.g., rivers, mountains).
        2. Demographic or other human boundaries (e.g., the community ends along a religious or linguistic barrier—in the community people speak Italian and attend a Roman Catholic church, while across the street people speak Greek and attend an Orthodox church).
        3. Official boundaries (e.g., governmentally sanctioned town or township lines).
    B. What specific factors make this community different from others in the same vicinity?
    C. What factors link the community to others in the same vicinity?
    D. What are the facilities for getting to and around this community?
        1. Transportation.
        2. Communications (telephone, telegraph, short-wave, drum beats, whistles, smoke signals).

II. Entering the community
    A. Are special arrangements needed to enter the community?
        1. Permission of the local sheriff's office or chief of police.
        2. Cooperation of village elders.
        3. Passports and visas (if out of the country).
    B. What is the best way of getting to the community (fastest and least expensive)?
    C. Is there some time of year when it is better to arrive than any other? If so, why?
    D. What special clothing or other equipment will be needed for living here for an extended period?
        1. If special clothing or equipment is necessary, should the fieldworker bring it with him, or is it cheaper and/or more readily available in the community itself?

III. Establishing the researcher in the community
    A. Whom should he contact first?
        1. Officials.
        2. The social leaders.

3. The ordinary folks.

B. If you think it would make a difference to contact one or the other of these immediately, explain why.

C. Is there anyone to avoid initially?

    1. Groups.

    2. Individuals.

D. Explain why these people should be avoided.

E. Where should residence be established?

    1. Buy own home?

    2. Rent home, or apartment, or room?

    3. Board in someone's house?

        a. With a single person or family?

        b. With what kind of people?

F. How should he explain what he is doing?

G. Should he seek work in the community as a "cover" for his research?

    1. If so, why and what kind? If not, why not?

    2. Should he join, or attend the meetings of, local organizations (churches, clubs, etc.)?

H. Should he (she), if single, date local women (men)? If so, why? If not, why not?

I. If the community is large and has many people living in it, whom should he seek out to be his key informants? Why? How should they be chosen?

    1. How would he best cultivate their friendship and cooperation?

        a. Should informants be given a regular salary? Periodic gifts? Or would any giving be considered inappropriate?

            i. If something needs to be given, what is the best thing to give (money, food, favors)?

IV. Methodology

Assuming that the researcher has no one specific area of culture he wishes to study more intensively than any other:

A. Discuss in some detail the data-gathering techniques you would use to give him "depth in view" coverage of the community. You may use those discussed in this book, or devise ones you think would be more appropriate to the local situation.

    1. Are certain techniques more appropriate to use for certain people than for others? If so, why?

    2. Are certain techniques more appropriate to use for collecting certain types of data than others? If so, why?

(In answering these questions, be very specific about how the research is to be carried out. That is, do not say "Study attitudes by means of a questionnaire." Say a few words about what type of questions to ask, when to survey, whom to survey, how and when to pretest, etc.)

B. Are there any situations in which using a camera or a tape recorder would be considered either offensive or otherwise inappropriate? If so, why? How would you compensate for this, if necessary?

C. In describing your research techniques, be sure to include some notation of what kinds of equipment are necessary (camera, film, tapes, measuring devices, or whatever). Also take note of the question of data recording: how should field notes be kept and stored? How is it best to organize them for efficient retrieval?

V. Leaving the community

A. Should he report to anyone officially about his departure plans?

B. Should he give going-away presents to informants in the field?

1. Should he expect many going-away presents from his informants, and if so, what should be his proper response to such generosity? (That is, will he be expected to continue to reciprocate even after leaving the field?)

VI. The post-field period

A. How should he organize the analysis and writing up of his data?

B. Presuming it is advisable for the community to be aware of his analysis, should he seek their approval before having it published? If so, whom should he ask? How?

C. Once it has been published, how should he disseminate copies to members of the community? How many? To whom?

D. Add any other comments about the conduct of the field study in your community that you think are particularly appropriate to the local situation.

If you like, you may do this project as a group effort. Suppose that you were approached to plan a Steward-type study of aspects of American culture. Several people in the class could then discuss the study of their own communities in the context of "American culture" (or a regional subculture, if that is more appropriate). In this case, you would have to be very careful about standardizing your methodology sections so that the studies would be comparable. You could also do a Smith/Clarke study on a specific topic: for example, the comparative study of family organization in selected American communities.

SELECTED ANNOTATED BIBLIOGRAPHY

Arensberg, Conrad M.
   The Irish Countryman. Macmillan, 1937. The original version of this classic community study.

Arensberg, Conrad M.
  "The Community Study Method." *American Journal of Sociology,* 1954, 60:
  109–24. A concise summary of some of the methodological and theoretical
  points raised in this chapter.
Arensberg, Conrad M.
  "American Communities." *American Anthropologist* 1955, 57:1143–62. An
  application of Arensberg's community study method to a classification of
  types of contemporary American communities.
Arensberg, Conrad M.
  "The Community as Object and as Sample." *American Anthropologist,* 1961,
  63:241–64. Sets forth the major theoretical premises of the approach.
Arensberg, Conrad M., and Solon T. Kimball
  Family and Community in Ireland. Harvard University Press, 1940. Their clas-
  sic study.
Arensberg, Conrad M., and Solon T. Kimball
  Culture and Community. Harcourt, Brace and World, 1965. A compendium of
  various theoretical, methodological, and descriptive articles written by these
  two pioneers of the community study approach.
Barker, Roger G.
  Ecological Psychology. Stanford University Press, 1968. The detailed survey of
  the theory and method involved in the study of interpersonal interaction
  within a community framework.
Clarke, Edith
  My Mother Who Fathered Me. London: George Allen and Unwin, 1957. A
  frequently cited comparative study of three Jamaican communities with
  regard to their respective organizations.
Hollingshead, August B.
  "Community Research Development and Present Conditions." *American So-
  ciological Review* 1948, 13:136–46. A concise history of the community study
  approach, focusing mainly on sociology, but with reference to anthropology
  as well.
Lynd, Robert S., and Helen M. Lynd
  Middletown: A Study in Contemporary American Culture. Harcourt, Brace,
  1929. The classic study of a United States community.
Pilcher, William W.
  The Portland Longshoremen: A Dispersed Urban Community. Holt, Rinehart and
  Winston, 1972. A readable account of a contemporary United States com-
  munity, noteworthy for its focus on a group defined by shared participation
  and common interests rather than geographic proximity.
Redfield, Robert
  Chan Kom: A Mayan Village. Carnegie Institution of Washington, 1934. One
  of the pioneering studies in the anthropological approach to community
  study, and a classic ethnography in its own right.
Redfield, Robert
  The Little Community. University of Chicago Press, 1955. The theoretical
  foundations of Redfield's approach to the community study.
Smith, Michael G.
  "Community Organization in Rural Jamaica." In Michael G. Smith, ed., *The*

Plural Society in the British West Indies, 1965. Although the examples in this volume are Caribbean, the book is an important contribution to both the theory and the method of community studies, particularly in the so-called "plural societies" of the modern world.

Smith, Raymond T.

The Negro Family in British Guiana. London: Routledge and Kegan Paul, 1956. An analysis of three communities in British Guiana (now Guyana), comparing variations in kinship and domestic organization.

Steward, Julian

Area Research: Theory and Practice. Social Science Research Council Bulletin 63, 1950. Contains a good section on community studies, as well as a thorough summary of the theoretical and methodological considerations underlying the Puerto Rico project.

Steward, Julian, et al.

The People of Puerto Rico. University of Illinois Press, 1956. The massive ethnographic end-product of the community study research undertaken by Steward and his colleagues.

INDEX

surveying for, 34
urban, 28, 35, 39
Maps
cadastral, 30
copyrighted, 32–33
Marrett, R. R., 96
Material culture, 18, 54, 60, 97
photographing, 161, 173
Maya, 180
Mayer-Oakes, W. J., 102
Mead, M., 64, 66, 74–75, 157, 161
Mexico, 18, 35, 38, 54, 159, 180
Michelson, T., 78
Middle East, 24, 35, 39, 104
Middletown study, 178
Modern societies
folklore in, 113–114
formal organizations in, 144, 145
kinship in, 42
status and role in, 147–148
Modernization, 90–91, 153
Mormons, 89
Myths, 65, 106–107, 115
defined, 106–107

Naipaul, V. S., 110–111
Native categories
color terms, 124–125
eliciting, 53
emic vs. etic, 121–123
kinship, 43, 49
and map making, 29
See also Ethnosemantics
Narrative accounts, *See* Personal documentation
Navajo, 89
New Guinea, 6, 29, 54, 75
Naven ceremony in, 54
Newman, P., 6
Nigeria, 136
Norms
community, 178
and folklore, 108, 109, 112, 116
Notes and Queries in Anthropology, 5, 12
Nuer, 15
Nyoro, 90

Objectivity, 67, 68, 70
Ojibwa, 64–65

See also Chippewa
Observation, 18–19, 22, 69–70
and photography, 158, 162
Oral tradition, 106–109, 113, 115
Orenstein, H. M., 145
Outline of Cultural Materials, 12, 26

Participant observation, 22, 63–72, 182, 183
concept of, 63–64
and ethnocentrism, 60, 65
history of, 64–66
in a religious setting, 67–72
and selection of informants, 56, 75–76
Pelto, P. J., 56
Pentecostal churches, 69, 71
Personal documentation, 85–94
diaries as, 86
essays as, 86, 87–92
poems as, 91
and the study of values and attitudes, 86–87, 89–92, 94
See also Essays; Life histories
Philippines, 29
Pilcher, W. W., 184
Phonemics, 122, 123–124
Phonetics, 121
Photographic equipment, 59, 162–172
and interviewing informants, 59
light meters, 170–171
selecting, 162, 164, 166–167, 171
See also Cameras; Film; Photography
Photography
aerial, 32, 159
of artifacts, 173
of a building, 173
cautions about, 158–159, 187
depth of field, 167–168
ethics of, 158–159
history of, 157
and informant relations, 157–162
of an interior, 174
in map making, 32
of material culture, 161, 173
of nonverbal interaction, 161–162
parallax error, 164–165, 173
portraits, 173–174
prints, negatives and transparencies, 169–170